HOW TO BE KIND TO YOURSELF

A GUIDE TO NAVIGATING LIFE'S DAILY CHALLENGES WITH SELF-COMPASSION, SELF-ACCEPTANCE, AND EASE

HANNAH BRAIME

INDIVIDUATE PRESS

© 2022 Hannah Braime

All rights reserved. This book or any portion thereof may not be reproduced or used in any manner whatsoever without the express written permission of the publisher except for the use of brief quotations in a book review.

Individuate Press

CONTENTS

Introduction — v

PART 1
FEELING

1. How to Be Kind to Yourself When Your Inner Critic is on a Wild Rampage — 3
2. How to Be Kind to Yourself When You Feel "Not Good Enough" — 8
3. How to Be Kind to Yourself When You're Experiencing Envy (and Other "Bad" Feelings) — 18
4. How to Be Kind to Yourself When "Self-Love" Feels Unrelatable — 23
5. How to Be Kind to Yourself When You're Feeling Overwhelmed — 27
6. How to Be Kind to Yourself When You Don't Like How You're Feeling — 37
7. How to Be Kind to Yourself When You're Feeling Blue — 40
8. How to Be Kind to Yourself When You're Tired And/or Sick — 46
9. How to Be Kind to Yourself When You're Feeling Scared — 52
10. How to Be Kind to Yourself When You're Experiencing FOMO (the Fear of Missing Out) — 63
11. How to Be Kind to Yourself When You Feel Broken — 68

PART 2
DOING

12. How to Be Kind to Yourself When You Make a Mistake — 73
13. How to Be Kind to Yourself When it Feels Like You Have No Self-Control — 81

14. How to Be Kind to Yourself When You're Lacking Confidence — 86
15. How to Be Kind to Yourself When You're Setting Big Goals — 94
16. How to Be Kind to Yourself When You're Finding It Hard to Get Motivated — 101
17. How to Be Kind to Yourself When You're Too Busy for Self-Care — 110
18. How to Be Kind to Yourself When You're Struggling to Make the Changes You Want to Make — 121
19. How to Be Kind to Yourself When You Don't Do What You Say You're Going to Do — 137
20. How to Be Kind to Yourself When It's Hard to Detach Self-Worth from Productivity — 141

PART 3
BEING

21. How to Be Kind to Yourself When You Feel You're Lacking Purpose — 149
22. How to Be Kind to Yourself When the Urge to People-Please is Strong — 158
23. How to Be Kind to Yourself When You're Struggling to Balance Self-Acceptance & Self-Improvement — 163
24. How to Be Kind to Yourself in the Middle of Big Transitions — 169
25. How to Be Kind to Yourself in the Face of Judgment — 176
26. How to Be Kind to Yourself in the Face of Rejection — 183
27. How to Be Kind to Yourself When Bad Things Happen — 193
28. How to Be Kind to Yourself When Life Feels Like it's Falling Apart — 203

What Comes Next? — 207
Thanks for reading this book — 209
Bibliography — 210

Also by Hannah Braime	214
About the Author	215

INTRODUCTION

> Being human is not about being any one particular way; it is about being as life creates you—with your own particular strengths and weaknesses, gifts and challenges, quirks and oddities.
>
> —Kristen Neff, *Self-Compassion: Stop Beating Yourself Up and Leave Insecurity Behind*

When do you find it hard to be kind to yourself?

When I disappoint someone and I feel I'm not meeting their expectations of me.

When I'm looking at my naked body, or buying clothes.

When I see the many interconnected problems of the world and feel guilty I'm not doing enough.

When I think I've made a mistake.

When I give in to my social media addictions instead of doing a long list of things I enjoy more.

When I look at my finances.

When I hurt the ones I love (even if it was an accident).

When I lose my temper with my kids.

When I get dumped.

When I can't control aspects of my personality that others find off-putting.

When I choose to apologize for something that isn't my fault.

When I've overloaded my schedule.

After a social interaction in which I struggled to belong.

When I fail to meet a goal I have set for myself.

When my body/brain aren't behaving.

When I'm not being productive.

These are real responses to the above question. Perhaps you can relate to some of them; perhaps you can relate to all of them. You probably have a few additional answers of your own. Depending on your history, personality, and perspective, the experiences above might arise every now and again, or they might be part of your daily life. The truth for most of us is this: self-kindness is a constant work in progress. And, contrary to what most of us are taught, it matters.

Imagine you are going about your day—out for a walk, picking up some groceries, emailing at work—when out of the blue, *pfttt!*, an arrow strikes you in the arm. Your arm is on fire from the inside out, and you clutch at the area, uttering a few choice exclamations. Your mysterious assailant then steps out of the shadows and gives you a choice: do you want to be hit by a second arrow, or would you rather have the chance to heal?

It's a no-brainer: healing all the way. But now imagine this first arrow is an emotional rather than a physical pain. It's a difficult life event, a challenge, or an issue; it's arguing with your spouse or kid; it's losing your job; it's finding out you have a serious illness. This arrow also hits you at random, and it also hurts—in a different but equally painful way. And you have the same choice in this situation, except this time you are holding the bow with the second arrow.

This second arrow is your reaction to the first arrow. It's your judgment, criticism, or self-recrimination. It's beating yourself up, blaming yourself, allowing your inner critic to take over and run the show. You don't need to shoot this second arrow (the first arrow is painful enough). But this is what most of us do by default. Instead of further hurting ourselves with the second arrow and layering pain upon pain, we can choose to begin healing. This is where self-kindness comes in.

The tale of the two arrows is a Buddhist parable that illustrates the saying "Pain is inevitable, suffering is optional." Rejection, judgment, mistakes, comparison, self-doubt, feelings of insecurity—these experiences are an unavoidable part of life, and they all challenge our self-kindness when we need it most. If you're reading this book, you probably understand that self-kindness is important. Perhaps you are good at showing yourself kindness in your daily life. But understanding it's important and actually practicing it when our self-compassion is most tested is another matter entirely.

That's where this book comes in: to offer support and encouragement during those times it's hardest to be kind to ourselves. One of the tricky things about self-criticism is that it feels like we're alone. There is something wrong with us, everyone else has their emotional life sorted, and we're the only ones messing up or feeling messed up. In reality, most of us struggle with self-kindness in different situations, on different days, and when faced with different difficulties. My intention in writing this book was to create a place to go for comfort, support, and perspective when you feel most challenged. Each chapter takes a situation where being kind to ourselves can be hardest and offers guidance and suggestions I hope will support you as you encounter these challenges.

The chapters in this book are organized into three sections: feeling (common challenges related to our emotions), doing (situations that might challenge our self-kindness as we live our days and get things done), and being (times when existing as a person in the world feels hard). While I encourage you to read it all the way through, you are welcome to choose the chapters that sound like they'd be most helpful to you right now. At the end of each chapter, you'll find "Your moment of self-kindness," which is one or more questions that encourage you to reflect on how to use the ideas in the chapter in your own life. As someone who has read a *lot* of personal growth books, I know there is a big difference between reading about ideas and concepts, and actually putting them into practice. These questions bridge the gap between theory and real-life application, and I encourage you to take the time to respond to these questions and make connections between what you've just read and how you can use it in your life.

Think of this book like a collection of ideas you can dip into when you need a different perspective from the one your inner critic offers, and a few suggestions about how to be kind to yourself when you are hurting the most. Because however much you try to avoid painful emotional experiences (and believe me, I have tried!), they are part of life, part of being human, and something that is ultimately out of our control. What we can control: how we respond in those moments, starting with how we respond to ourselves. Instead of firing the second arrow, we can choose compassion, kindness, and healing. This book is a reminder to choose the latter.

I'm aware in writing this book that I am one person, with one set of experiences and my individual lens through which I see the world. You are coming to this book from a different place and background, with a unique set of experiences and perspectives. So I invite you to take what works for you and leave what doesn't. Some questions and concepts in this book might be uncomfortable to explore. They might bring up heavy or unexpected thoughts or feelings, or you might feel stuck and unable to change the internal feedback loop you're hearing to one that is kinder on your own. I invite you to approach these sections in whichever way feels most helpful to you and only go as deep as you feel comfortable going. This book is not any kind of substitute for professional support; there are a variety of helping professionals out there who are great at what they do and want to support you. If you have an inkling that might be helpful and the means to do so, I hope you'll make use of them.

Happy reading and stay kind to yourself,

Hannah

P.S. As well as the Resource list you will find at the end of this book, I've created a living resources page for *How to Be Kind to Yourself* that has direct links to all the book recommendations and resources I mention throughout this book. You can find that here: http://www.becomingwhoyouare.net/htbk-resources.

PART 1
FEELING

ONE

HOW TO BE KIND TO YOURSELF WHEN YOUR INNER CRITIC IS ON A WILD RAMPAGE

Self-acceptance is my refusal to be in an adversarial relationship with myself.

—Nathaniel Branden, *The Six Pillars of Self-Esteem*

Over the last few years, it's become popular to dismiss our inner critics, to empower ourselves by fighting back and playing them at their own game.

My inner critic is such a jerk.

Don't listen to your inner gremlins.

That mean girl inside your head: ignore her.

Oh, that's just your inner asshole talking.

I'm sure the inner critic needs little introduction. This is the voice (or voices) inside our head that tells us how we're falling short, screwing up, not good enough, and so on, ad nauseam. The negative effects of our inner critics are real. They can undermine our sense of worth, confidence, self-acceptance, hurling our past and present transgressions at us until we feel like a walking bundle of flaws and issues. They are almost impossible to control, no matter how hard we try—and believe me, I've tried. There is a special frustration and fatigue that comes with a vocal inner critic, saying nasty things to you day in, day out. It's soul-destroying, and telling it where to get off can feel bold! Empowering! Like you're taking back control!

But that's when the self-war really starts.

I've tried the name-calling I described above. I've tried to put this voice in its place, to show it's met its match. But if I want to turn this into a fight, the odds are already stacked against me. My inner critic will always out-shout, out-argue, and out-maneuver me in psychological games. If someone in my external life is following me around, heckling me 24/7 with vicious and unfair observations and critiques, I have a choice: get nasty back, try to reason with them, crumble, or put a physical boundary between myself and that person. The latter is usually the best option, especially when all other reasonable responses have been exhausted. But when it's me saying those things to myself, there is no leaving.

I've also tried ignoring this voice. I've tried to pretend it doesn't exist, that it doesn't bother me. I've tried listening to positive affirmations that tell me *yes, I am a beautiful flower, inside and out! I am worthy of love and belonging!* But behind these words is my inner critic, chanting, "Wrong! What about that stupid thing you said six years ago? Or that time you made a fool of yourself in public? Or all these mistakes you've made (FYI, it's a *long* list so we're going to be here a while…)."

A friend who is a former therapist described how he had a choice whenever he was in a session with a client: he either allowed the client to pull him into their world or he encouraged the client to step into his. The same dynamic applies to our inner critics. We can lower ourselves—our behavior, communication, standards—to their level. We can shout back, name-call, say things about them that are as nasty as the things they say to us. Or, we can encourage them to rise to our standard and model what fair, compassionate communication looks like.

The solution to self-criticism is never more criticism. Of ourselves, or of our inner critics.

So what is the solution?

Compassion, yes. *My inner critic says these things to me and I want to understand why. When I imagine myself saying those things to someone, I recognize it comes from a place of fear and hurt.* You know compassion is important. But knowing this and practicing it are two very different things. Sometimes compassion feels a long way away, too far out of reach. When that's the case, I prefer to go for acceptance. Acceptance isn't the same as liking, but is about being able to acknowledge the reality of what is without judgment: *When my inner critic says these things to me, I feel hurt.* And when that feels too far out of reach? We can practice being an impartial observer: *This is happening.* We can pay attention to the thoughts running through our head, the feelings those thoughts provoke, and what we want (or don't want) to do in response. This isn't about judging or changing what's happening, but about adopting an air of curiosity and "Huh, that's interesting." It's about noticing that these pieces all fit together in a jigsaw of "Stuff I'm still working on (and that's OK)."

Many years ago, I heard author and artist Leonie Dawson talk in an interview about what people want—really, truly want. She said, and I paraphrase, that it boiled down to wanting someone to see us for all and everything we are and say, "I hear you, I see you, and I understand you." I don't know about you, but I think the person it is most difficult for me to say these words to with sincerity is myself, including my inner critic.

So I start with one piece at a time.

OK, inner critic, I hear you. I don't agree with you; I don't accept what you're saying as de facto truth and I'm not buying into these stories you're selling, but I will not fight you anymore.

OK, inner critic, I see you. I see beneath your anger, vitriol and incessant nagging, and I see fear. A deep well of fear and scarcity that has nothing to do with me as a person and everything to do with your beliefs about the world and my place in it. Here, I'm giving you back these beliefs because they belong to you. I see you as a part of me, and I also see that you don't represent me as a whole.

OK, inner critic, I understand you. I see you trying to keep me small, hidden, sticking to the rules and the script. To you, this is safety. I see that deep down you're trying to protect me from the things you fear the most: rejection, abandonment, external criticism, and other psychological threats.

These pieces are not set in stone. Sometimes I need to stop and ask myself: *how would I want to be treated if I were having a tough time? If I were mired in fear and anxiety?* When I respond to my inner critic, this is me responding to a part of myself. So it's my responsibility to treat myself how I want to be treated.

If you'd like to explore this topic further, I invite you to check out my book, *The Power of Self-Kindness: How to Transform Your Relationship with Your Inner Critic.* In the meantime, the next chapter deals with a related topic: how to be kind to ourselves when we feel "not good enough."

Your moment of self-kindness:

How do you want to be treated by others? And how does this translate into how you treat yourself?

What would this treatment look like if you were to extend it to your inner critic?

How would the way you think about your inner critic shift if you tried to raise it to meet you instead of sinking down to its level?

TWO
HOW TO BE KIND TO YOURSELF WHEN YOU FEEL "NOT GOOD ENOUGH"

Most of the shadows of this life are caused by standing in one's own sunshine.

—Ralph Waldo Emerson

When I reflect on the biggest thoughts, beliefs, and feelings that have held me back in life, "I'm not good enough," is the winner, hands down. I used to think the fact I was thinking "I'm not good enough" was a sign that I wasn't good enough. People who are actually good enough don't think that way, right? So I went to war with this belief, armed with the conviction that eventually I'd reach a point where I wouldn't feel self-doubt. In the meantime, though, the existence of this thought was a sign of how far I had to go until I was "fixed."

Spoiler alert: this hasn't happened (yet). I still experience self-doubt, and I sometimes still feel not good enough, especially when I compare myself to certain people or in certain situations (oh, hi, social media!). But like a lot of the internal experiences discussed in this book, I've also come to realize I don't need to wait for these thoughts to disappear to live the way I want to live and be the person I want to be. While it's tempting to tell the "not good enough" narrative to get lost, I've learned these thoughts can contain an important message:

1. I'm avoiding something important, or I'm not adequately prepared.

In the previous chapter, "How to Be Kind to Yourself When Your Inner Critic is on a Wild Rampage," I mentioned it's not kind to ourselves to ignore our inner critics outright. Here's another reason: although how our critics express themselves isn't helpful, sometimes their feedback contains nuggets of truth. If that's the case and this feeling is highlighting where I can improve or do better, that's important, too. But, as I'll share in the next few pages, the aim is not to be the best, but my best.

2. This situation is an opportunity for growth.

Noticing where and when I'm telling myself I'm not good enough helps me unpack the stories behind that statement. It's an opportunity to revise false and unhelpful beliefs. It's a chance to question whether the way I see myself reflects who I actually am.

In this chapter, I want to explore two of the biggest driving forces behind this "not good enough" belief: comparison and perfectionism. I'm addressing them together because they are connected. No doubt you've experienced what it feels like to compare yourself to someone else and feel less-than. But perfectionism is also a kind of comparison. We put this ideal, superhuman version of ourselves next to the reality of our current selves, compare, and despair. The outcome of both? Not good enough.

We experience this when we go to that art class we've wanted to take and realize that everyone else is streaks ahead of us. We finally decide to sit down and write the novel we've been thinking about since forever, only to stop because we're writing at the level of "The cat sat on the mat," while other people are producing masterpieces. We decide this is the year we're going to get our finances in order, only to glance at our bank statement and dissolve into a funk about how terrible we are at adulting compared to most people.

One of the biggest lessons I've learned over the last couple of years is not to compare myself to people who are several years ahead of me on a particular life path, including paths that involve them discovering a certain approach or way of life years earlier than I did. After all, you don't know what you don't know while you don't know it. It's not fair, it doesn't help me, it doesn't serve what I'm doing at that moment (whether that's work- or life-related), and it's a primer for "not good enough." Instead, I try to focus on what I can learn from these people. I use the experience of comparison to learn more about my needs, what I want my life to look like, and how I want to feel.

The truth about "good enough"

Everyone starts from the beginning.

Being a beginner at something can be tough. It feels awkward and unnatural, it's uncomfortable and it challenges our ego. But everyone starts as a beginner in everything. Whenever I'm finding it hard to be a beginner,

I think about babies. When babies learn to pull themselves up and walk, it takes them many tries before they make it happen. The first time a baby falls down, do they sit back, think "Oh well, guess I'm not cut out for this whole 'learning to walk' thing after all," and never try again? No: they get back up and keep going over weeks, even months, until they succeed. The same goes for talking, fine motor skills, and everything we've learned to do since then. You were once that baby, which means you've already mastered some epic skills that take an enormous amount of practice, coordination, and understanding. Whatever challenges you're facing now, adopt the same tenacity you've used to overcome other challenges and learn new skills in the past, and remember how much you've already accomplished.

Other people's successes do not take away from us being enough in our own lives.

Life as a path is a well-worn metaphor, but bear with me because it's worth repeating. You are walking your path. Other people are on individual paths of their own. We're each trying to get to where we want to be using the path we have, and the path we are on differs from the path someone else is walking, with different curves, undulations, obstacles, and short-cuts.

If someone else achieves a goal we want to achieve, that doesn't mean we are a failure, we've missed our opportunity, or we're never going to do that. It just means they've reached a certain point on their path that still lies ahead of us on ours. Equally, other people's choices don't define whether we are good enough in our own lives: only we can do that. There will always be people who appear to be more successful, more popular, more wealthy, and more (insert trait here) than us. As the famous saying from Steve

Furtick goes, "The reason we struggle with insecurity is because we compare our behind-the-scenes to other people's highlight reel." This is especially the case in the age of social media.

So how do we say bye-bye to comparison? Well, we can't. You've probably heard the advice before to just stop comparing yourself to other people and found that's a lot harder to do than it sounds. Comparison is one of those built-in systems that historically has helped our ancestors survive and got us to where we are today. It's something we are drawn to do, whether or not we like it. Comparison can even be helpful when we use it in the right way, but it's something we need to approach with care.

The golden shadow

When my eldest child was two, my husband and I put down some roots after traveling during the few years before that. As part of setting up our new home, I wanted to create a dedicated play space for my daughter. I took to the Internet for inspiration and a few Instagram accounts later was feeling small and overwhelmed. These kids had Aladdin's Caves of toys, beautifully organized into something that more resembled a work of art than friends' cluttered playrooms I remembered from my childhood. Their mothers seemed to spend all their free time creating elaborate play scenes, finding novel ways to stimulate their kids with sensory experiences, and furthering their development. What kind of mother was I if I wasn't providing my child with a color-coordinated selection of hand-carved wooden toys each morning? Or lighting a candle and reading her poetry last thing before bed? Or going bird-spotting and foraging for mushrooms? I hadn't gone into this exercise feeling my parenting was lacking, but now I was deep in "not good enough." When I slowed down and thought through what I was feeling, I realized that underneath the surface there was something I wanted to emulate from these pictures—not things, but intention. What appealed to me about all these pictures and captions, and the meaning they held for me, was these people were all intentional about how they spend time with their kids. They thought about their children's experiences and wanted to create beauty and engagement for them. I loved this approach, and wanted to do the same, but in a way that aligned with my values as a parent and my daughter's interests.

One reason we compare ourselves to others is they reflect our own unacknowledged potential or our own unmet needs and desires. This is something psychologist Carl Jung described as "the golden shadow." When you look at someone and thinking, "I wish I could do that too," part of you is drawing your attention to the fact that you could do it too. So... why aren't you?

Sometimes there are valid reasons or, as in the case above, it might be that "doing it too" means doing it in our own way. But sometimes these comparisons also point to things we could do but aren't doing because of an outdated story or unhelpful belief we are holding onto. As in the situation I described above, sometimes our comparison isn't what it seems to be about, either. It might take some exploration to dig down and discover exactly what the unacknowledged and unlived desire is. Either way, rather than chastising yourself or simply dismissing your comparison, stop and ask: "How does this comparison reflect what I'm not owning in myself? What is this telling me about my own unacknowledged potential?" The answer might surprise you.

Now we've explored comparison, perfectionism, and some different ways of thinking about it, how do you deal with these experiences when they come up? Here are a few things I've found helpful. I hope they are useful for you, too:

Ask yourself, "What's one thing I can do to move this project/passion/idea forward right now?"

Most of us believe that progress happens like this:

Step one: Find confidence.

Step two: Feel ready.

Step three: Take action.

The belief we need to feel confident before we can take action comes from perfectionism. If you're doing something you've never done before, chances are you won't feel confident or ready, because you're doing something you've never done before. As I'll talk about more in part two of this book, confidence comes from action, not the other way around. That's where the question above is useful. The "one thing" you do doesn't have to be big. In fact, it's better if it's not in the beginning. It could be sending an email, reaching out to someone you know who can help, tidying up your CV, or looking at your budget. If you wait until you feel confident to start, you're going to be waiting for a long time. But with each small step, you'll find your confidence grows.

Focus on what you can do, rather than what you can't

When we're deep in comparison or perfectionism, we develop tunnel vision, focusing on the ways we're falling short, the things we can't do, and the opportunities to screw up. When you notice this kind of tunnel vision kicking in, take a mental step back and focus on what you can do and what is working. Rather than dwelling on all the things that might not happen or might go wrong, focus on what makes you the perfect person for this situation. Instead of focusing on trying to fix your weaknesses—perceived or real—invest that energy into focusing on your strengths.

Focus on being *your* best, rather than *the* best

As writer and entrepreneur Sarah K. Peck explained in an interview, "There's only one person who's the best in the world, and just look at the probability: it's probably not you. So we can get that out of our way." Out of 8 billion people in the world, we're unlikely to be the best at what we're doing, so we can relax!

Rather than focusing on trying to be the best (and beating ourselves up when we inevitably aren't), it's far more constructive and empowering is to focus on being our best. Instead of focusing on what everyone else is doing (or not doing), can we compare ourselves to ourselves this time yesterday, last week, last year, and look at how far we've come since then? Even this kind of comparison has its limitations. What looks like "our best" will change depending on the day, our energy, our health, factors and circumstances in life beyond our control. But at any moment, the only question that's important to ask ourselves isn't "Am I doing or being the best right now?" but "Am I doing or being *my* best right now?"

The answer to this question doesn't exist in external results, but in our internal barometer. Which is why it's important to…

Let go of the outcome

Feeling inadequate often comes from trying to control things we can't control, including what other people think of us. Even when we try our hardest, the result might still not be exactly what we'd hoped for. We often treat situations as though we have 100% control over them, when in reality there are plenty of external variables that contribute to the outcome. You can give a dazzling performance in a job interview, but the company might still go for another candidate. You might work really hard at your relationship, but the other person might still decide that they want something else. We have influence over these outcomes, but not control. Life becomes a lot simpler when we give up trying to control the things we can't control and start focusing our effort and energy on the things we can.

Letting go of the outcome isn't the same as not caring. I care a lot about many things: my health, my husband, my kids, my friends, my work, my financial security, and much more. What I have control over—and what I can pour my care into—is how I show up for these things. That's what doing my best is all about, and it's very different from trying to control a particular outcome. I use a mantra to help remind me of this balance, which comes from author and teacher Angeles Arrien: "Show up, Pay attention, Tell the truth, Let go of the outcome."

It reminds me of the approach I want to take across all areas of my life: dedication to the process without attachment to the outcome. In the next chapter, you'll discover how to practice self-kindness when you're experiencing envy and other so-called bad feelings. Before that, though, here are a couple of questions for you to consider.

Your moment of self-kindness:

How do you plan to respond next time you notice "not good enough" thoughts coming up?

Which of the alternatives above resonate with you?

THREE
HOW TO BE KIND TO YOURSELF WHEN YOU'RE EXPERIENCING ENVY (AND OTHER "BAD" FEELINGS)

Emotions can get in the way or get you on the way.

—Mavis Mazhura

We all experience feeling envy, jealousy, resentment, and other so-called bad feelings from time to time. Although they are pervasive in our culture (and part of being human), we're unlikely to acknowledge them to ourselves, let alone to other people. Admiration, celebration, gratitude—these are the emotions we're more likely to talk about. They can also become a bypass for some of the less acceptable feelings, the safe experiences we name when it's too uncomfortable to admit how we really feel.

But the reality is we can feel a mixture of contradictory feelings, all at the same time. We can be happy for someone's engagement and still feel a pang of envy about the happy and stable relationship we long for ourselves. We can see someone get a job, get promoted, win an award, and be happy for them, and still feel a longing for that kind of recognition and visibility ourselves. We can see someone's holiday snaps on Facebook, enjoy the beauty of them, and still wish we had the opportunity for more peace in our hectic lives.

And that's OK. The danger that comes with feeling envy and similar feelings is another thought riding alongside those dual emotions "... and if I can't have those things, I don't want that person to have them either." This is where feeling envy becomes destructive. This chapter is about how to turn these so-called bad feelings into a force for good. I'm focusing on envy as this is something we all experience, especially in the digital age, where social media posturing and comparison is rife. But the principles and reframes I share below apply to other hard-to-accept feelings, too.

First, if you've been telling yourself you shouldn't feel envy because envy is bad, here's the reality: envy is hard-wired. It's an evolutionary mechanism for survival. When our ancestors saw a fellow cave-dweller with an antelope they didn't have, they felt envy. As a result, they either deferred to the other cave-dweller as someone who possessed superior hunting skills, got rid of him and kept the antelope for themselves, or went out to get an antelope of their own. Envy is part of the reason you and I are here today.

Whether or not we like it, envy is an emotion and emotion drives action. And this is where we need to be mindful. Envy can be destructive, as I mentioned. The dark side of envy is that thought: *if I can't have this, no one else should be able to, either*. Unchecked, it can lead us to want to tear people down, to take away what they have. It leads to nasty gossip behind someone's back; it leads to doing things that try to make the object of our envy seem insignificant.

But envy can be a driving force for good—when we recognize and accept it. In Jungian psychology, we find the theory of the "Golden Shadow." This describes the unlived live(s) we have disowned in the past but still feel drawn to. It's the feelings, traits or qualities that we want to embody more in our own lives, the potential and the paths that call us. I already mentioned the theory of the Golden Shadow in the previous chapter. It shows up in the ways we compare ourselves to other people, and can be present in feelings of envy, too. Recognizing we are feeling envious can lead to fruitful self-exploration: *what is it that this person has that I want?* (Hint: this is usually less about material goods and achievements and more about what those things represent to us and how we want to feel.) *How do I imagine I'll feel when I have it? Where am I denying myself this thing right now? In what ways am I keeping it out of my life? And how can I meet this need in the future?*

Let's say Jill is listening to Bob talk about his glorious two weeks in the Bahamas and recognizes a creeping sense of envy. As she pauses and asks herself the questions above, she realizes the source of her envy isn't Bob's holiday to the Bahamas, but what she imagines is the experience behind it. She yearns for a greater sense of freedom in her life, and imagines Bob has the freedom to take such a trip without worrying about finances. As she explores it further, Jill also realizes she envies the quality time she imagines Bob having with his significant other on his trip. She craves that kind of time with her partner, which is difficult with their hectic schedules. Having identified her desire for freedom and connection, Jill thinks about how she can create opportunities to experience more of these things. She resolves to make time to explore all the different ways she could experience more freedom in her life. She also talks to her partner about spending more quality time together and planning something for them both to look forward to in the future.

Envy can be helpful with the enormous caveat it's helpful when we put that energy behind it to good use. What's not a good use? Writing nasty things about people online. Shaming someone for having more than we do. Downplaying people's wins and successes because they feel threatening. Trying to undermine someone else because we perceive them to be more successful, smarter, more attractive, or more [*insert trait here*] than us. Good use includes (but isn't limited to) identifying what's provoking envy: the need, the desire, the longing. Is it for love? To be seen? To feel like we matter? To feel useful? To feel worthy of taking up space? And then using that envy to renew our focus on our own patch of grass, on our own actions; looking at what's missing and how we're keeping it out. The experience of envy can feel counterintuitive because although it's directed toward someone else, it's nothing to do with them. It's a reflection of our own feelings about ourselves and our lives.

If you'd like to explore the roots of your envy in more depth, here are a few writing prompts you can use:

1. When was the last time you remember feeling envy?

2. What was the situation? Write the facts, leaving your interpretation out for now.

3. What was the story you told yourself at the time?

4. Getting as specific as possible: what provoked the envy? This is usually not something tangible, but more of a core need (you can use this list to help).

5. What stops you from meeting more of this need in your life?

6. How do you stop yourself from meeting more of this need in your life?

7. What is one thing you can do differently from now on to meet more of this need in your life?

The same principle applies to other so-called bad feelings (resentment, jealousy, and others). Our emotions might not always reflect the truth of the current situation, but they matter. Experiencing a feeling isn't right or wrong, bad or good: it just is. We can't control whether we experience a certain emotion. We can choose what we do with that feeling and how we respond to it, internally and externally.

I hope this chapter has helped you move toward acceptance of all feelings, even those that are uncomfortable in the moment. The next chapter is about a somewhat related topic: self-love (or struggles with it). If you need an extra dose of self-acceptance but struggle with the concept of self-love, I hope you'll keep reading.

Your moment of self-kindness:

Where do you most often experience envy in your life?

What feeling(s) or need(s) do you think could be behind this envy?

How do you usually respond to feeling envy?

How can you approach experiencing envy with greater self-kindness in the future?

FOUR
HOW TO BE KIND TO YOURSELF WHEN "SELF-LOVE" FEELS UNRELATABLE

> You are allowed to be both a masterpiece and a work in progress, simultaneously.
>
> — Sophia Bush

In the personal growth world, the term "self-love" is thrown around like confetti. Describing everything from self-care activities to a mindset of self-acceptance and compassion, it's hard to pinpoint exactly what self-love means beyond some kind of nebulous nirvana where we always feel good about ourselves and our place in the world. I don't know about you, but I've experienced self-love less as a state of being and more as a process. I've had fleeting moments of it, when I've felt at peace with myself and with the world. But then something happens: a thought pops into my head; my inner critic pipes up; I get tired, hormonal, thirsty; I remember something important I meant to do but didn't. And the nirvana disappears.

Here's the truth: I do not always feel self-loving, nor do I need to. Self-love can feel like a lot of pressure for those of us who have a more, let's say, complicated relationship with ourselves. This doesn't mean I believe the voice that tells me I'm not good enough or lazy, or that other people are thinking mean things about me. Not at all. Some of the times I am kindest to myself are when I feel least self-loving, because that's when I know I most need that kindness. Some of my deepest learning comes from the times when I struggle most with self-love, because those times are where the lessons lie. But I also don't need to wait for that voice to disappear, or to be 100% free of internal conflict, to create meaning, fulfillment, and happiness within my life. The risk of buying into the self-love hype is that we end up putting our hopes, aspirations, and desires on hold, waiting for the magical "when... then..." that will solve all our problems. "When I feel self-love, then I'll... change jobs/leave my relationship/start that project/go on that trip I've been thinking about/feel like I deserve nice things, etc."

The aim of personal development isn't to strive for perfection, nor is it to be some kind of superhuman. When I first became interested in personal growth, I was in a dark place and my goal was to get out of that dark place. I thought that would mean becoming immune to hurt, pain, frustration, ambivalence, uncertainty, discomfort, anger, rejection, and everything else we struggle with as humans. But this doesn't happen *because* we are human. As author Brené Brown explains in her book *Daring Greatly: How the Courage to Be Vulnerable Transforms the Way We Live, Love, Parent, and Lead*, when we try to shut out the uncomfortable experiences, we also end up shutting out joy, excitement, anticipation, bliss, hope, enjoyment, and all the things we crave. The aim of personal development and self-awareness is to open ourselves up to our feelings more. It's also to learn to respond to them, rather than react. Also, because we are human, our feelings don't fit into neat little boxes. We are capable of contradictions, which means we can love and loathe at the same time. We can feel happiness and sadness, insecure and loved, certainty and uncertainty, confidence and fear. All these feelings can co-exist, mingle, bounce off one another, and create a big feelings stew—and that's part of being alive.

So if the term "self-love" doesn't quite resonate with you either, that's OK. We're all works in progress making our own way in this world. I also want to clarify: this chapter isn't meant to be an implied criticism of people who do use and enjoy this phrase. If that's you and self-love works for you, keep doing what you're doing! What I want to explore and gently challenge is the notion that self-love is what we *should* all be striving for, and to introduce some alternatives.

Alternatives to self-love

Instead of self-love, I choose to focus on our humanness and everything that comes with it. I focus on the areas in which we have agency, responsibility (which, if you sound it out, becomes *response-ability*), and choice.

This includes *self-kindness*, which is a choice to show love, a conscious decision to behave lovingly toward ourselves.

It includes *self-care*, which is a choice to look after our physical, emotional and mental needs.

It includes *self-expression*, which is a choice to share our gifts and vision with the world, to give people on the outside a peek at what's going on inside.

It also includes *self-acceptance*, which is a choice to accept reality. This isn't the same as liking reality, but it gives us an opportunity to acknowledge what is true and real.

In summary, if you don't feel self-loving, that's OK. It doesn't mean you're failing at personal growth or there's something wrong with you. It just means your way of describing and thinking about your relationship with yourself is different. Self-kindness isn't a state of being we either have or don't have. It's a series of decisions and something we practice imperfectly daily. Whichever way we choose to describe our experience, the most important thing is that we show up each day ready to continue exploring, learning, and evolving.

In the next chapter, we'll explore self-kindness in the face of overwhelm. In the meantime, here are a few questions for you to reflect on.

Your moment of self-kindness:

How do you feel about the term self-love? Is it one that resonates with you, or does it leave you feeling slightly "off," even alienated?

Which of the alternatives to self-love could use your attention?

What are three small things you can start doing in your life to embody these alternatives?

FIVE
HOW TO BE KIND TO YOURSELF WHEN YOU'RE FEELING OVERWHELMED

Life should be touched, not strangled. You've got to relax, let it happen at times, and at others move forward with it.

—Ray Bradbury

Overwhelm can come from many sources and directions. It can result from big demands placed on us by external sources, or those we place on ourselves. It can come as the result of a sudden shock or unexpected change in life. It can be slow-burning, building bit by bit until we realize one day we're in way over our heads. Whatever the cause of the overwhelm, it's hard to be kind to ourselves when we have big events, commitments, and demands pulling our attention and energy in different directions. It's also hard when we feel stuck paralyzed, or on an emotional rollercoaster, unable to take the next step or reclaim control over the situation.

When I've felt overwhelmed, it's been because I was trying to do too much at once and/or trying to control circumstances I can only influence but don't have full power over. Like all feelings, overwhelm is a message. It's a potent reminder that, no matter how often we create careful plans, life happens and we are human. When I'm feeling overwhelmed but haven't yet realized I'm feeling this way, my go-to response is to *do*. I write to-do lists as long as my forearm, try to get more done in less time, and become a version of myself that is more akin to a robot than a person. But whenever I try to *do* first and *be* later, it doesn't work. Instead, I'm reminded of how important it is to stay kind to ourselves in the face of overwhelm and keep practicing the suggestions I want to share with you in this chapter.

Stop, just for a minute, and breathe

We cannot make good decisions when we're feeling overwhelmed, nor can we operate at 100%. So stop for a minute, close your eyes and take several deep breaths. When we're stressed, we engage the sympathetic nervous system, a branch of our autonomic nervous system that puts us in fight-or-flight mode. Physical signs our sympathetic nervous system has been activated include rapid, shallow breathing, and an increased heart rate. Because our rate and depth of breathing is something we can influence, we can use this as a tool to activate another component of our autonomic nervous system. This is the parasympathetic nervous system (also known as the "rest and digest" part of our nervous system). Slowing our breathing helps take us from the fight-or-flight response to the calmer domain of the parasympathetic nervous system. Long, deep breaths help calm our physical selves and send reassuring signals to our nervous system. This has a direct impact on our emotional state, too.

Accept how you feel

You'll notice this is a common theme throughout this book: accept your moment-to-moment experience. This repetition is intentional. Even though I know self-kindness is rooted in acceptance, I need regular reminders to acknowledge my feelings and experience rather than trying to change them. Feeling overwhelmed is no exception. When I'm in this place, I chivvy myself: "Come on, other people do all of this and more; snap out of it!" The implication I shouldn't feel overwhelmed only makes me feel worse about the fact I do. This increases my stress levels and therefore my overwhelm. A kinder option involves remembering two simple truths:

1. **All feelings are transitory.** The good and the bad, they are all like riding a wave. Some waves are more turbulent than others and can leave us feeling like we're no longer steering the ship, but the storm will calm. What we're experiencing right now might not feel pleasant, but it, too, will pass.
2. **Everyone feels this way at some point.** When we're experiencing overwhelm or another hard emotion, it can feel lonely. Everyone else is doing great, right? No, they aren't, and these kinds of thoughts only compound our misery. We all have better and worse ways of dealing with life, and even the most seemingly unruffled person experiences overwhelm in certain situations.

Check your beliefs

Sometimes our overwhelm isn't a result of what's happening in our lives so much as how we're thinking about what's happening in our lives. Our beliefs have a huge impact on how we see the world, and this can work both for and against us. Research by Professor Richard Wiseman, as outlined in his book *The Luck Factor: The Scientific Study of the Lucky Mind*, has shown that people who believe they are lucky are luckier. This isn't down to some mysterious universal force, but because they are more likely to notice opportunities to be lucky. Equally, people who believe they are unlucky are unluckier. Again, this isn't because the universe has dealt them a bad hand, but because they aren't open to evidence and opportunities that would contradict this belief. The result is that they are less likely to see the opportunities to be lucky when they arise.

Common beliefs that can contribute to overwhelm include:

- **Negative self-beliefs: "I'm not capable of doing this."** As above, if we believe something to be true about ourselves, we will act in a way that reinforces that belief—good or bad. If part of you is saying, "You're not capable of doing this," you're more likely to behave as though this were true. Try shifting this kind of belief by asking yourself a question like, "How could I do this?" "What's the first step I need to take?" or, "What needs to happen for me to do this?"
- **Superhero syndrome: "I have to do this all myself."** No, you don't. I'm all too familiar with this belief and know from experience it does more harm than good. Rather than independence, try

embracing in*ter*dependence. Recognize there will be times when you'll benefit from having external support and help, just as there will be times when you can offer support and help. Asking makes you stronger, not weaker.

- **"No" aversion: "If I say no, people will be unhappy with me."** Perhaps, but that's their response and therefore their responsibility. A request that comes without the possibility of saying "no" isn't a request, it's a demand. No one will care about our needs and wellbeing for us. When people make requests, they're looking out for their needs and wellbeing. When we say no, we're looking out for ours.

- **All-or-nothing thinking: "It either has to be perfect or there's no point in starting."** It's healthy to hold ourselves to high standards, but all-or-nothing thinking is self-sabotage. Instead, repeat this phrase to yourself: "progress over perfection." As we talked about in the previous chapter, if you're starting out with something, you won't be good at it. To get to the part where you become good, you need to go through the part where you're bad at it first. That's how you'll improve. Practice focusing on the process rather than the outcome. Concentrate on giving activities your full effort, while letting go of any expectations about how they need to turn out. In most situations, we don't have full control over how a particular situation evolves. The only thing we have control over is our contribution. Focus on that, and try to enjoy the ride.

- **Self-identification: "I'm always so overwhelmed!"** Thoughts like this can become a self-fulfilling prophecy. When I believe this, I buy into the idea I am "an overwhelmed person" and seek beliefs and situations that reinforce this identity. Instead, we can accept how we feel without adopting that feeling as part of our identity. Experiencing overwhelm is fine. It happens to all of us, but that's not where we stop. The next question is: "What am I going to do about it?"

Get out of firefighter mode

When we're engaged in a constant struggle to stay on top of things, we end up in firefighter mode. Here, we spend our days responding to immediate emergencies and deadlines—the little fires of our daily lives. These are the things we need to do right now before it's too late, the things we forgot to do earlier, or the things we meant to do before but didn't. One or two of these is easy to extinguish, but several at once can feel like they are burning down the house.

If you've experienced this, you'll probably know this way of dealing with life isn't good for us in the long term. It's stressful, it affects our personal and professional relationships (especially if we're in the habit of telling people we'll do things then not doing them; we'll talk about this more in part two), and makes it much easier for things to slip through the cracks, adding even further overwhelm to the pile.

For some of us, this is the only way of life we've known and it's difficult to imagine an alternative. But it is possible and starts with one (rather unglamorous-sounding) solution:

Routines and systems

Routines and systems might sound boring and impersonal, but they are about making life as easy as possible. If I know I will clear my email inbox by a certain time each Friday, I don't have to worry about unanswered emails anymore. If I have a place to store all my to-dos and I set up a time to review them each week, I don't need to keep them all in my head. If I decide in advance when I'm going to do crucial self-care activities like exercise and schedule it into my calendar, I don't need to remind myself to do it each day. If I can't take on a particular engagement or activity without sacrificing another one that is more important, I don't. No more frequent apologies to people for not following through on commitments. No more waking up at 2am with a ticker of forgotten deadlines running through our heads. No more deprioritizing the activities that help us feel like the best version of ourselves. How good would that feel?

For an excellent introduction to systems that help you stay out of firefighter mode, I recommend *Getting Things Done: The Art of Stress-Free Productivity* by David Allen. You can find a list of other helpful tools in the Resources page for this book.

Change your language

One of the leading causes of overwhelm is saying "yes" when we want to say "no" and over-committing. We can get a pretty good gauge of the things we've wrongly committed to by replacing the phrase "have to" with the phrase "choose to."

This is a subtle shift but by noticing how we feel when we say "I choose to clean my flat every Saturday morning" and "I choose to see that friend who talks non-stop about her breakup from two years ago and never asks about what's happening in my life," we can identify which commitments it's time to release and take more self-ownership for honoring the rest.

Out of everything we do in life, very few things are "have to"s. A few of these include basic functions like breathing, sleeping, eating, and using the bathroom. The rest is all stuff we choose to do. Yes, that includes going to work, laundry, and taking your kids to sports practice. You have the freedom to turn around and say "I'm not doing that."

True, you'll face consequences, like losing your job, having dirty clothes, and unhappy children (and/or coaches), but that doesn't mean you *have* to do those things. You choose to do them because you like the consequences of doing them. You like having money (and hopefully get some kind of fulfillment from your job), you prefer wearing clean clothes to soiled, obnoxious-smelling garments, and you prefer seeing your kids burn off some energy and have fun on the field rather than get frustrated and bounce off the walls at home.

This is a subtle but important distinction. It's the difference between feeling resentful, frustrated and victimized, and feeling grateful, liberated and empowered.

Another mantra I've found helpful to remember is, "When I say yes to something, I am saying no to something else," and vice versa, "When I say no to something, I am saying *yes* to something else." Although it's something I'm working on and improving, I still struggle with the "no aversion" I mentioned earlier. I worry about hurting the asker's feelings or disappointing them, I worry they will judge me, I worry about missing out, and I start second-guessing myself and thinking thoughts like "Well, I *could* do this thing, so maybe I should...". This has led me to say "yes" to things and then regret it later far more often than I've said "no" and then regretted it. Viewing these situations through the lens of this mantra helps me stay mindful of what I'm saying "no" to when I say "yes" to something else. Time with my family? Time to work on my own projects? Peace of mind? Much-needed alone time? Money I could contribute to my savings account?

Being mindful of everything I am saying yes to and everything I am saying no to helps me make decisions that are better-aligned with my priorities and prevents me tipping from busy into overwhelmed.

Start by putting one foot in front of the other

How do you run a marathon? You put one foot in front of another, again and again, until you reach the finish line. Easy, right?! But this is how you do it. This is an apt metaphor for most situations in life, especially those that leave us feeling overwhelmed. In these kinds of situations, I find it helpful to think of my journey like an adventurous hike or a long-distance run, and focus on the very next step. Once I've taken that step, then I can focus on the next step after that, the next after that, and so on. Bringing our focus down from 30,000 feet to what's immediately in front of us and identifying just one action we can take, right here, right now, enables us to take that all-important first step without becoming paralyzed. This approach has helped me write books, tackle international moves, transition to self-employment, start a business, and more.

Sometimes, overcoming overwhelm is a question of mindset and reframing how we're looking at our lives. How we think and talk about the commitments and activities that make up our days matters. Sometimes, however, it's not enough to think ourselves out of overwhelm; we need to *do* something (or some things) differently too. This might look like renegotiating commitments. It could involve dropping a few non-essential activities. Perhaps it looks like taking ownership of how we spend our time, making hard decisions, and having tough conversations.

We can change our minds. This is where self-kindness isn't one-size-fits-all. Behaving in a flakey way is not self-kindness; over time, that flakiness corrodes our sense of self-trust. Part of figuring out what self-kindness looks like for us is to tell the difference between those commitments we need to honor (to maintain our sense of integrity, to honor our relationships), those we don't, and how to bow out graciously and make amends for the latter.

Whatever it looks like to you, getting out of overwhelm starts with taking that single first step. It might feel like an insurmountable task and like you have an ultra-marathon ahead of you. But the only thing you ever need to do is focus on the very next step ahead, then the one after that, then the next, and keep going.

Your moment of self-kindness:

Which situations provoke overwhelm for you?

How do you usually respond when you feel overwhelmed?

How would you like to respond?

Which of these suggestions do you think will be most helpful to you in times of overwhelm?

How are you going to use it next time you encounter this situation?

SIX
HOW TO BE KIND TO YOURSELF WHEN YOU DON'T LIKE HOW YOU'RE FEELING

To experience peace does not mean that your life is always blissful. It means that you are capable of tapping into a blissful state of mind amidst the normal chaos of a hectic life

—Jill Bolte Taylor

Although we all know we should accept our feelings, sometimes that's easier said than done. Our emotions can be deeply uncomfortable, even akin to physical pain. In those moments, it's tempting to want to push them down, numb them, and do whatever we can to not have to feel this way.

It might be a cold comfort in the moment, but take heart from the fact that if you're feeling down, then you're *feeling*. We can't choose our emotional experiences. As Brené Brown writes in *The Gifts of Imperfection,* "We cannot selectively numb emotions; when we numb the painful emotions, we also numb the positive emotions." If we allow ourselves to feel the lows, we also open ourselves up to feel higher highs too.

As I mentioned in the previous chapter, we are not our feelings. When we think or say things to ourselves like "I am sad," "I am angry," or "I am lonely," we are more likely to self-identify with those feelings. A more accurate way of describing our experience is to say "I *feel* sad," "I *feel* angry," or "I *feel* lonely". Remember, all feelings are transitory, so they don't define us. When we use "I feel..." instead of "I am...," we're still acknowledging the feeling, but we're not labeling ourselves into a corner.

Feelings are not states of being; rather they come and go in waves. They're in constant flux and are temporary at their core. When we're in the middle of a low period, it can sometimes feel like it won't end. We fear being trapped, feeling this way forever. I used to avoid so-called bad feelings for fear of being swallowed up by them. But if we allow ourselves to feel feelings, however strong, the act of letting them wash over us usually lessens their intensity. Trying to avoid them has the opposite effect.

Our feelings will lift. Sometimes it's so imperceptible we don't realize it's happened until later. But it will come. And if it doesn't? Our emotions are here to tell us something. They're rich with information from the past and the present. Perhaps your emotions are telling you it's time for some extra support. Perhaps they are highlighting something that needs to change. Maybe they are pointing to an unmet need, maybe all the above.

Every emotion is acceptable. Yes, our culture has ideas about how certain feelings are bad, even wrong, but as we'll explore later in this book, this isn't true: feelings in themselves aren't right or wrong, they just are. It's what we do with them and how we respond to them that counts. So welcome them to join you as temporary companions on your journey. Don't let them take the wheel, but don't shove them back into the trunk, either. Instead, allow them to be a passenger as you travel to your next destination. The next chapters follow on from this topic, starting with how to be kind to ourselves when we're feeling blue before moving onto treating ourselves kindly when we're tired or sick, feeling fear, experiencing fear, and feeling broken.

Your moment of self-kindness:

What feelings are you struggling to accept in yourself right now?

What would be different if you could feel more acceptance toward them? How would you feel? How might it impact your daily life?

SEVEN

HOW TO BE KIND TO YOURSELF WHEN YOU'RE FEELING BLUE

Courage doesn't always roar. Sometimes courage is the quiet voice at the end of the day saying, "I will try again tomorrow."

—Mary Anne Radmacher

Maybe you've had a falling out with someone, maybe things aren't going well at work, maybe you've had hard or disappointing news, maybe you can't figure out why… Whatever the cause, this chapter is all about how to be kind to yourself when you're feeling blue. Before we start, I want to clarify that the suggestions I share in this chapter are for dealing with times when these feelings are fleeting. Feeling blue is not the same as having depression in the clinical sense, which—among other symptoms—is characterized by feeling sadness, hopelessness, or emptiness every day for at least two weeks. In this situation, the kindest thing you can do for yourself is to seek support from a doctor, qualified therapist, or other appropriate source.

Even when they are fleeting, though, these feelings can have a significant impact on our quality of life, and a little self-kindness can go a long way…

Remember that everything passes

As we've touched on in the last two chapters, feelings are transitory, and chances are that you've felt this way before. I mention this here again because when we're in the middle of a challenging or uncomfortable emotion, it can be hard to see beyond how we're feeling right now. I experience a few days of feeling down and it feels like this is it, this is just how I will feel from now on. But that hasn't yet become truth. Instead, I can usually trace these feelings back to needs: needing more sleep, needing connection with others, needing to reconnect with my sense of purpose and meaning in life, needing to wait a couple of days for hormones to settle, needing to take a break from parenting/work/all the things. Once I've identified what those needs are, I can do something about them. The highs and lows we experience each have their own arc; some last longer than others, but they all shift into the next feeling at some point.

Some days we'll feel on top of the world; other days we'll feel like we're squinting up at the tiny speck of light way off at the top of our dark hole. Most days, we'll be somewhere pretty neutral. But it all moves, shifts, and eventually passes, if we're willing to give ourselves space and time and accept our own process.

And if the feelings don't pass? As I mentioned above, if you notice you're feeling blue or hopeless over a longer period of time, it's worth reaching out to a professional to get some additional support. That's self-kindness, too.

Here are a few questions you can use when you need a reminder that this too shall pass and things will get better again:

1. *Think of five times when you've felt most joyful and write down what you were doing, who you were with, and how you felt.*
2. *Think of five times when you've felt most fulfilled and write down what you were doing, who you were with, and how you felt.*
3. *Think of five times when you've felt safe and write down what you were doing and who you were with.*

Repurpose your energy

I've tried many things over the years to turn my frown upside down. These include listening to music, raiding the fridge, taking a nap, going for a walk, and many healthy and not-so-healthy things besides. However, there's one thing, without fail, that helps me get back on my feet: paying it forward.

Having run a website and blog for 10 years, I am lucky to have received many kind, generous, and supportive messages during that time. One drawback of sharing anything online though is the not-so-kind interactions. It's tempting to spend hours ruminating over a negative message or critical review. Realizing this wasn't a good use of my time, I started paying it forward—not through being shirty with someone else (!), but by turning that around and doing something more constructive. I go online and leave a positive book review for an author I enjoyed recently. I send someone who has inspired me a thank-you message. I think of something nice to do for a friend or colleague. I reach out to someone I haven't spoken to for a while to see how they are doing. And afterwards, unreasonable emails don't matter so much anymore.

Since then, that has been my go-to method for turning myself around, whatever the situation. Energy can't be created or destroyed, it just changes—and we can make that change. Negative energy in, positive energy out. When I'm feeling an influx of negative energy, I figure out how I can turn it into something positive or good, and I use that energy and drive to do that.

Try this: What is one act of kindness you can use to pay it forward?

Ask for support (and be specific about what kind of support you want)

Sometimes we talk to people because we want their feedback, advice, and suggestions. Sometimes we talk to people because we want to be seen, heard, and understood. It's an act of self-kindness to identify the type of support we want and to communicate that to the other person. When we're clear with ourselves about what we need, we're far more likely to get it.

What often happens in conversations is we talk to someone (or they talk to us) about a situation, problem, or issue they are facing, and the other person jumps in with well-meaning and often quite useful advice... that falls flat as a pancake because it's not advice we want. Most of our problems are figure out-able (or at least Google-able). Usually, when we share a problem with someone, we want that someone to say to (or show us), "I see you, I hear you, I understand you." We want empathy. My husband and I have had many conversations about this and, after repeated discussions in which we missed each other completely, we have agreed to say "I'm not looking for advice right now, I would just appreciate you listening/giving me a hug," or whatever we need in that moment.

Try this: What kind of support do you need when you're feeling blue? How can you request this?

Create a self-kindness kit

Being kind to ourselves when we're feeling blue can be challenging. When we're already in that place, we might feel stuck, listless, uncertain, and not really in a position to be creative and problem-solve. So, prepare. If you know you're going to be experiencing challenges over the next few weeks/months/years, get ready in advance. The kit is a list of go-to activities that represent self-kindness when things get tough. Your kit can be multi-sensory. It might include something that smells nice, a childhood toy, quotes of meaningful things people have said to you, a list of your favorite movies or TV shows, local places you can easily visit, and more. Think of the things that put a smile on your face and bring them together for a quick pick-me-up when you're feeling blue.

You can find a guide to creating your own self-kindness kit on the resources page for this book.

Try this: What would you add to your self-kindness kit? Make a list now so it's ready for when you most need it.

Start a "When Life Works" list

A When Life Works list is a list of the activities and practices that help us feel at our physical and emotional best. They might include things like getting enough sleep, drinking enough water, exercising, connecting with nature, meditation, or a wide variety of other possibilities. Some non-negotiable activities on my list are journaling, exercising, reading, and spending time outside, but the specific activities themselves aren't as important as how they make you feel. Not everything on your When Life Works list will be fun. I don't always want to do these things (see: exercise), but I know that however much resistance I have, I will feel a thousand times better after doing it than if I don't.

Once you've identified what these activities are, make time to do these things first each day. Even if you only have a few minutes. Your When Life Works list is the foundation of your self-care and self-connection, and it doesn't have to take up hours of your time. I've found I have a very different experience of my day when I take just 10 minutes to do some reflective writing in the morning. If you'd like help to identify the activities and practices to add to your When Life Works list, you can download a free worksheet to help you identify your own non-negotiables on the Resources page for this book.

Try this: Which activities or practices would go on your When Life Works list?

Your moment of self-kindness:

Which of these suggestions do you think could be most helpful to you next time you're feeling blue?

What would it look like to be 10% kinder to yourself next time you're having a tough day?

EIGHT
HOW TO BE KIND TO YOURSELF WHEN YOU'RE TIRED AND/OR SICK

Having compassion starts and ends with having compassion for all those unwanted parts of ourselves, all those imperfections that we don't even want to look at.

—Pema Chodron

Long-term exhaustion, chronic illness, even a short-term bout of something nasty... so far in this book, we've covered how our emotions can affect our levels of self-kindness. But our physical feelings can affect how we feel about ourselves, too.

Exhaustion and illness are two of my biggest personal barriers to self-care. I find it hard to ask others for help and to give myself permission to slow down. I don't make good decisions, and I get frustrated with myself for not functioning at 100%. The result is that I can end up feeling miserable, anxious, and overwhelmed.

In my early twenties, I was diagnosed with endometriosis. This gynecological condition causes intense pain, fatigue and a range of other unpleasant effects. I'm lucky to have a mild version, but it still affects me. Learning to go with the flow (pun intended) and be kind to myself, whatever my body throws at me, has been challenging but crucial.

Chronic illness, fatigue, injury, and similar are huge topics that fill many books of their own. I am not an expert on this topic, nor can I do them justice in one chapter alone. However, I also don't want to ignore the effect physical ailments can have on our relationship with ourselves, as it matters deeply. Here are some lessons I've learned about how to be kind to ourselves when we're feeling sick, exhausted and done:

Recognize that there is no "right" way to feel about it

Our physical state affects our emotions. Some days we might feel optimistic, ready for action, and inspired. Others, we might feel drained, sad, and frustrated. Arguing with reality doesn't change reality. How you feel on any day doesn't matter as much as *accepting* how you feel.

I've found expecting my feelings about the situation to ebb and flow to be helpful. While I do what I can to take care of my mental health and practice optimism, I also acknowledge that some days I don't feel optimistic. I feel like crap, and I feel resentful, despairing, and the rest of the day stretches ahead of me, feeling interminably long. Those feelings are OK, too. If I tell myself I should feel grateful, it's not that bad, plenty of people go through this, and so on, I'm firing that second arrow we talked about in the introduction to this book and making an already difficult situation harder.

Practicing a neutral and detached observation of our feelings when we're feeling rough isn't always a fair or realistic goal. Instead, I've found it helpful to normalize the complex web of emotions that can come with physical ailments using thoughts like "I feel X *and* I feel Y." I feel frustrated and I feel hopeful; I feel exhausted, over it, and I'm glad it's not worse. All feelings allowed, all feelings valid.

Remember: being sick or tired isn't a flaw

We live in a culture that values hustle, productivity, and doing. While there is nothing wrong with those things—in fact, they are all forces for good in the right context—the hustle worship can come with a darker subtext: if you don't behave like this, you are less valuable. This is nothing new; it's yet another example of the "better than/lesser than" paradigm that infiltrates our society. But when you're getting bombarded with messages every day that being busy equals good and not being busy equals bad, it's hard not to buy into this story. From pithy quotes on social media ("Don't wish for it, work for it!" "Your only limit is your mind!"), to the general expectation of rapid-fire email, direct message, and on-demand everything, things happen faster than ever before, and we are expected to happen faster than even before, too.

Illness, health issues, and exhaustion challenge that paradigm. Even when our minds are still in go-go-go mode, our bodies can put a hard stop to any plans we might have, pushing mandated rest to the top of our to-do list. And this can leave us with all kinds of feelings, from FOMO to much deeper and insidious fears.

When we experience health challenges, it's easy to question whether there is something wrong with us, deeper than a physical or emotional condition. We feel flawed. People around us who don't understand, or have misperceptions about, our experience often exacerbate this without meaning to.

Sometimes, we all need a reminder that being sick or tired isn't bad or good—it just is. When we're tired, we're tired. When we're sick, we're sick. It is what it is, no extra meanings or judgments required. And if it feels hard not to be "productive?" Try reframing rest and taking care of yourself as being the most productive thing you could do at that moment.

Reflect on whether there's anything different you could do next time to prepare

If you've been working yourself to the bone and, as a result, are completely exhausted and getting sick all the time, what needs to change? If you know certain things make a chronic illness worse, how can you avoid them? Don't wait until you reach emergency status to look after yourself. Consistent care is the key to avoiding emergencies and enjoying a better quality of life.

This can also involve planning around fluctuations in our physical wellbeing. If you have to take a trip into town and you know it will be exhausting, plan some downtime for the next day. If you know you feel fatigued and foggy during your period, try to make allowances for this and, where possible, plan ahead.

I wrote about the power of the When Life Works List in the last chapter, and it's something I'd encourage you to try. When life works and you feel great, what things contribute to that? And when life *doesn't* work, what contributes to that? Understanding the things that are already working (and not working) will help you develop creative habits that support and nurture your physical and mental health.

Compare and despair

Other people's experiences and decisions are not the same as ours, nor are they a reflection of our worthiness. If certain things (ahem, social media) or people are triggering the "compare and despair" response, I recommend returning to my chapter "How to Be Kind to Yourself When You Feel 'Not Good Enough'."

Ask yourself: what is the kindest thing I can do for myself right now?

I love this question as a self-care reset. It's simple and shifts my focus away from self-criticism to self-compassion. So what is the kindest thing you can do? Is it to nap? Great. Is it to watch a movie? Fab. Is it to acknowledge you feel tired and/or sick but also that you'll feel a lot better when you plow through that task that's hanging over you then relax, knowing it's done? Also fine.

Another question that's also relevant here is: *What is my future self most going to thank me for?* It might be rest and relaxation, it might be mustering your energy to see your current commitments through. It might be something in between. Only you know the answer, and asking is the first step to cultivating a more nurturing relationship with yourself.

Your moment of self-kindness:

What is the kindest thing you can do for yourself today?

What will your future self most thank you for?

If you experience chronic illness, flare-ups, or know you have regular times when you feel sub-par physically, what can you do when you are feeling well and more energetic to prepare for these?

NINE

HOW TO BE KIND TO YOURSELF WHEN YOU'RE FEELING SCARED

F-E-A-R has two meanings: "Forget Everything And Run" or "Face Everything And Rise." The choice is yours.

—Zig Ziglar

When I look back at some of the most positive opportunities, decisions, and changes in my life, one thing is clear: they have all been punctuated by fear. Fear of uncertainty, change, regret, failure, and even fear of success have stopped me from doing the things I want to do at one point or another. This chapter is about self-kindness in the face of fear. It's not about becoming fearless; after all, it's fear that stops us crossing the road when a bus is thundering our way. I want to feel fear in that kind of situation, because that fear keeps me alive. Instead of trying to eradicate our fears and anxieties, we're going to explore the different ways we can deal with them. I'm including anxiety in this chapter because fear and anxiety are closely related. They do, however, have nuanced differences. One of these is that fear is usually about specific things we know and understand (events, situations, outcomes, people, illnesses, etc.), while anxiety is around more unspecified situations or outcomes that aren't familiar or that we don't fully understand.

Before we begin, I want to clarify this chapter is about fear we experience in situations like trying something new, stepping outside our comfort zone, or taking an emotional risk—situations that feel scary, but in which we are physically safe. If that's not the case, then self-kindness looks like removing yourself from the situation (if possible), or reaching out for support. Safety is a fundamental human right.

Identifying your flavor of fear

Situations that feel emotionally threatening often evoke the same fear as situations that pose a physical threat. In our rational minds, we know we're not in physical danger when we step onto the stage for a public speaking engagement, but we sure feel like we could be.

Being kind to ourselves when we experience fear starts with identifying: is this a real-life threat? or is it more of an ego or emotional-based threat? Situations that could involve rejection, vulnerability, or doing something that takes us outside our comfort zone fall into the latter category. Once we recognize what we're feeling is emotional fear, our next step is to get to know this fear so we can both honor it and use its energy to our advantage.

In her book *Playing Big*, coach and author Tara Mohr describes two kinds of fear using terms from biblical

Hebrew: pachad and yirah. Pachad is "Projected or imagined fear." This activates the "lizard brain," the part of our brain responsible for our most basic reactions, including our fight-or-flight response. In a split second, without even knowing why, we get ready to run, to fight back, or we become paralyzed and unable to think or act. This is the fear that leaves us feeling like we are facing mortal peril when asking someone out on a date or we sing in front of an audience for the first time. Yirah is a different flavor of fear. This describes the fear that invites us to step up, grow, and take up a larger space than we were before. It's an energizing fear, and one we usually associate with exciting new possibilities and opportunities. It's "the fear that overcomes us when we suddenly find ourselves in possession of considerably more energy than we are used to, inhabiting a larger space than we are used to inhabiting." These fears do not exist independently of each other; often, we experience a combination of the two.

As you might already know from experience (I do), trying to eliminate our fear doesn't work. Instead, we can learn to work with our fear, rather than against it. This starts with figuring out which parts of our fear are pachad, and which are yirah. Here are some questions that can help put our fears into perspective:

Ask: Who will benefit from what you're about to do?

Nine times out of 10, my fear is to do with my ego. This question helps me get past that and step outside my comfort zone. Whatever we're working toward, it's easy to become focused on extrinsic rewards. This includes external motivation, like awards, accolades, certificates, and achievements. When we focus solely on this, however, we can overlook our internal motivators. This includes needs this activity might meet and values it fulfills. Intrinsic motivators might also include who we could help, who we could inspire, and what kind of message we're sending through our actions.

Ask: In 10 years' time, will I even remember this?

Nothing helps ease short-term fear like long-term vision. When I ask myself the question "How am I going to feel about this in 10 years' time?" the answer is usually "I'm going to be glad I tried," or "It won't even be a blip on my radar."

This perspective helps me recognize that, although I'm feeling intense fear right now, that feeling won't last forever. Whatever the outcome, there will always have new opportunities and projects.

Remember your gifts (and that it's allowed to be easy)

When I feel fear, I'm usually focused on all the reasons I can't do something, rather than all the reasons I can. This is a human trait: we are wired to be problem-solvers, and this has been a helpful survival mechanism for thousands of years. When we face situations that don't involve mortal danger, however, this mechanism can work against us.

It's also easy to overlook our gifts and talents because they're staring us in the face. After all, these are the things that feel natural to us, even easy. They are the things we don't have to think twice about. It's easy to assume that, because they feel this way to us, they feel that way to everyone. We don't realize that what comes naturally to us might feel challenging to someone else. As a culture, we have this belief that "easy" is somehow bad and, if we want something in life, we need to struggle for it. Talent alone only gets us so far and we need to work. But look for the skills and traits that feel natural to you and embrace them.

Remember past times when you felt your fear and did it anyway

When we feel afraid of something, we tend to develop tunnel vision and focus on the situation in front of us. Next time you encounter fear about a particular situation, think of the times when you've faced similar challenges. Recall what worked for you then and how you dealt with that situation in the past.

Finally, remember that fear and excitement often feel the same within our bodies; they just show up in a different context and with different thoughts behind them. By embracing yirah and treating our fear with kindness, while also honoring our capabilities and strengths, we can transform our experience of fear from something to be avoided into something to be welcomed.

Calming fear and anxiety over an upcoming event

A few years ago, I needed to have surgery. It was minor enough to be a day-patient procedure but major enough to need general anesthetic—the prospect of which provoked a fair degree of fear and anxiety. Before this point, I had never had surgery or even broken anything more dramatic than my little toe, so the idea of being unconscious while people cut me open left me feeling totally wigged out (*hello, fear*). Add to that the fact I had a four-month-old baby (which brings up all the feels about the uncertainty of life, mortality, and the future), and I was also anxious about the whole event.

After a few nights of waking up at 2am to nurse my daughter, then lying awake for the next two to three hours feeling stifled by a heavy sense of dread, I knew I had to calm my nerves. I know I'm not alone in experiencing this kind of anxiety about upcoming events where much is out of our control. And I know facing these events head-on is part of life. Here's what has helped me in these situations. Whatever you're about to face (or might face in the future), I hope these suggestions are helpful for you too:

Research

Many of my fears came from the fact I knew nothing about surgery, beyond TV shows where people seemed to stop breathing dramatically during otherwise routine surgery (*ahem, Grey's Anatomy*). Learning more about how the process worked and reading up on statistics helped give me a far more realistic perspective. This option isn't for everyone and I know people who find it more comforting to take the "ignorance is bliss" approach, but I prefer to know what I'm facing head-on. I will research risks, options, and every aspect of something I'm anxious about until I feel like I have a handle on it. Here, my research on confirmed what my rational mind was telling me: the surgery would be fine, I would be fine, and in a few months I'd look back at the whole event knowing there was nothing to worry about (which is exactly what happened).

What information are you missing about the source of your anxiety? Where can you find it? Who can you talk to in order to feel more informed?

Practice negative visualization

Although we usually avoid thinking about the worst that could happen, why not let yourself go there? My worst-case scenario was that I would die, which was unlikely given it wasn't major surgery (and, as I knew from my research, the odds were incredibly low even if it were). After a couple of weeks of telling myself not to be so melodramatic (which, funnily enough, doesn't help), I allowed myself to contemplate my worst-case scenario without shutting down that train of thought.

Even though it was uncomfortable, it actually helped me feel calmer. The worst-case scenario with *everything* is: we die. And, although dying is a bummer, as Marcus Aurelius wrote in *Meditations*, it's not like we will feel anything or know we're dead, so what is there really to be afraid of? The most useful thing we can do right now is stay in the present and savor what there is to savor.

What is your worst-case scenario? Write out everything you think could go wrong and face it.

Focus on what you can control

Most of the things we dwell on are out of our control. Ruminating on my surgery gave me a false sense of power, as though my thoughts (and how long I spent thinking about them) could somehow change fate. Of course, this wasn't the case. Focusing on the things we can control is helpful, focusing on the things we have no power over or ability to change, not so much.

When I was focusing on things I couldn't control pre-surgery, I found I was distracting myself from focusing on the things I could. Shifting my focus to the things I had control over helped me feel more at peace about the things I didn't.

Create two lists: one of everything you can control in this situation and one of everything you can't control. Are you spending your time focusing on the right list?

Do something from your When Life Works list

I already talked about creating a When Life Works list in the chapter "How to Be Kind to Yourself When You're Feeling Blue," but I raise it here too because it's also useful when preparing to face anxiety-inducing situations. This list is a fundamental part of my self-care because it works. If you haven't already made your list, consider this your friendly reminder to return to that chapter and do it.

Enjoy the small moments

To quote author Dani DiPirro, "Focus more on what *is* than what *if*." This might seem like it contradicts negative visualization, but these two practices work together. Rather than trying to shove away negative thoughts and focus on the positive, give yourself a chance to let them happen. Take what you can from it—an appreciation of the present—then move on to focusing on what is.

What would you do differently if you focused more on what is than what if?

Breathe

It's simple, and it works. As I already mentioned in "How to Be Kind to Yourself When You're Feeling Overwhelmed," slowing our breathing helps take us from fight-or-flight response to the calmer domain of the parasympathetic nervous system. This affects our emotional wellbeing, our physical body, our thinking, and decision-making abilities. Calming our breathing when we're feeling fearful or anxious has obvious benefits.

Take a big deep breath to the count of five, then exhale all the way to the count of seven. Repeat this four to five times and notice the difference in how you feel.

Think of times you've faced a similar challenge in the past and it's turned out OK

While this might be the biggest, most anxiety-provoking obstacle you've faced yet, it's still helpful to remember previous times you've encountered uncertainty, doubt, and fear, and to think about how you handled them. Not only does this help us look at lessons from the past, but it can also bolster our confidence in our ability to handle the future.

When have you faced a similar challenge? What worked? What didn't? And how can that inform how you approach this event now?

Share your fear

On surgery day, as I walked up to the theater, the nurse asked me how I was feeling. I said I was nervous. He said he understood. He had recently had five (!) surgeries to remove a stubborn kidney stone and everything had been fine each time. Hearing his story reminded me: people do this all the time. I am not alone in what I'm feeling, and more often than not, everything goes well.

Who can you share your fear with? And what do you need from them? Reassurance? Understanding? Advice? Have a clear request in mind and share.

Explore the beliefs underneath the anxiety

I noticed I felt more anxious after becoming a parent. Part of that came from having far more responsibility. Part of it was hormones (so many hormones). Part of it also stemmed from buried beliefs about myself and my life that no longer served me.

At the time I was having all this anxiety, things were great. Being a mother was far more rewarding, fun and, in some ways, easier than I thought it would be. Things were going well in my relationship, we had exciting plans for the future; I was in good health (except the reason behind the surgery), and I was slowly finding a balance between parenthood and other aspects of my life and identity that were also important to me.

And while this was all going on, part of me was waiting for the other shoe to drop, for the catch. This part struggles to believe things could be this good without some kind of karmic re-balancing coming my way. It latches on to anything it can feel anxious about and runs with it. Everything is fair game.

Even though I've been doing this kind of self-reflection and self-work for over a decade (and I'm in a very different place in my life than when I started), it still feels vulnerable to allow myself to feel happy. I have to remind myself that things are good, right here, right now, whatever the future holds.

I don't think beliefs around deserving/not deserving to be happy are at the root of all anxiety (although I'm sure they play a role for some people). But the beliefs we have about ourselves and our lives are powerful. The more we notice our beliefs and the sway they hold over our lives, the more we can decide which we want to hold on to, and which it's time to discard.

Your moment of kindness:

How do you usually respond when you feel anxious and/or scared?

What has helped you when you've felt this way in the past?

What hasn't helped? What, on reflection, can you remove from your toolbox of responses?

How will you respond with kindness and compassion the next time you notice yourself feeling scared or anxious?

TEN
HOW TO BE KIND TO YOURSELF WHEN YOU'RE EXPERIENCING FOMO (THE FEAR OF MISSING OUT)

> Fear of missing out (FOMO): "A worried feeling that you may miss exciting events that other people are going to, especially caused by things you see on social media."
>
> —Cambridge English Dictionary

Even if you're not already with the term FOMO, you've probably experienced it. A group of friends plan a weekend away together that you can't go on. You spot a deal for that thing you've been wanting for ages—except quick; it expires in five minutes. Everyone you know seems to be making in-jokes about a new TV show—that you haven't seen.

As an adult, I've noticed FOMO seems to arise around specific needs. For me, it's connection. I see Facebook friends posting pictures of themselves laugh-hugging at conferences and, to part of me, suddenly it seems like it would totally be worth paying thousands of dollars I don't have, dealing with the upheaval and jet-lag, and traveling halfway around the world just for a two-day event that would be exhausting and not enjoyable for this introvert. For some people, it's things like visibility, recognition, and/or acceptance. They see a colleague or friend posting in a big online publication and fear they're slipping behind. They see friends getting married, buying houses, having babies, traveling, and their life feels somewhat mundane in comparison.

Most of all, the thing I've noticed most about fear of missing out is that it's not just about missing out. Depending on the context, it's also tied to envy, a fear of regret and a sense of not quite being or having enough. If you've read the previous sections of this book, you'll notice how all these experiences are symbiotic. We don't experience only one of them in isolation; there's usually a smattering of several others in there too.

As much as I love certain aspects of this hyper-connected world we live in, I'm also aware it can become one big vicious cycle of FOMO. Social media, in particular, is a breeding ground for FOMO. We feel the temptation to edit our lives, posting only the most flattering photos, the coolest links, and the most like-worthy updates. We also see other people doing the same, which further fuels our urgency to produce flattering photos, cool links, and like-worthy updates. And so the cycle continues. Marketers are also wise to the power of FOMO and use it to their advantage. "FOMO marketing" is part of the marketing lexicon and describes different techniques and tactics that play on this emotional experience. This is nothing new (marketing is all about persuading people to buy or do things through ethical and not-so-ethical means), but as we discuss FOMO, I feel it's important to acknowledge that promotions, adverts, and platforms evoke FOMO because that's one of the big things that keeps us—the consumers—coming back. If you experience FOMO, it's not because there's something wrong with you, it's because the user experience is designed to make you feel that way.

So how do we deal with fear of missing out? I've found there isn't a single "cure" that will stop FOMO in its tracks and prevent it from returning for good. Instead, it's a combination of being mindful, aware, and accepting of our moment-to-moment experience. Here are a few things I find helpful when FOMO takes hold:

Slowing down and looking for the underlying needs

Fear of missing out usually comes with urgency, which can lead us to make poor decisions. It's somewhat ironic that in trying to avoid regret, we end up doing things that leave us more likely to experience regret. Whenever I experience FOMO, I know that's a good signal to slow down and take a step back before I react hastily to the situation.

A 2013 study on FOMO suggested people who experience fear of missing out regularly have unmet psychological needs for competence, autonomy, and relatedness. I've started viewing my own episodes of FOMO as a cue that it's time to up my connection quota and take steps to meet that need myself. Usually this doesn't involve doing the thing that provokes my FOMO in the first place, because it's not about that event or activity, it's about the root needs underneath. Once I acknowledge the need(s), the urgency dissipates.

Remembering that every day is another chance to do something different

Missed out on an exceptional dinner party? Host your own. Wanted to go to a great event but didn't find out about it until the last minute? Get a few of your favorite people together for your own workcation. See a friend making leaps and bounds with her career? Ask her how she's doing it.

Right now, as you're reading this, you're still here, still alive (and may it stay that way for a good long while!). That means even if you have a fear of missing out, you aren't missing out. You have far more opportunities to create what you want than you might even realize.

Embrace "JOMO"

Just because we can do something doesn't mean we should. We live in a world with more choices, opportunities, and connections than ever before, which is amazing but can also be a minefield. Just because we can watch our email inbox from waking until sleeping, put the latest and greatest smartphone on our credit card, or attend every social event we're invited to, it doesn't mean doing these things is a good idea.

This is where having a clear sense of our values can anchor us to what matters. A useful question to ask is: *"Is this going to bring me closer to, or take me further away from, what I want and who I want to be?"*

"JOMO", aka the Joy of Missing Out, is FOMO's much underrated counterpart. As a dyed-in-the-wool introvert, this has been one of my favorite aspects of addressing how FOMO shows up in my own life. Rather than feeling anxious about missing out on an opportunity, event, or social gathering, we can remember: sometimes it feels good to say no. In our hyper-connected YOLO world, there can be immense joy and satisfaction in deciding to slow down and focus on what's going on right here, right now, instead. One way this works for me is that I take frequent social media breaks. Rather than being bombarded by other people's wishes, preferences, and choices, I can focus on my own.

Connection is important, getting involved in something meaningful is important, seizing opportunities that matter is important, growth is important—but only when these things are motivated by joy, not fear.

Your moment of kindness:

In which situations do you feel FOMO?

How can you approach these situations with greater self-kindness in the future?

ELEVEN
HOW TO BE KIND TO YOURSELF WHEN YOU FEEL BROKEN

Embrace the glorious mess that you are.

—Elizabeth Gilbert

In my book *The Power of Self-Kindness: How to Transform Your Relationship with Your Inner Critic*, I talk about how the inner critic, like a typical abuser, is excellent at isolating us. It tells us that if only other people knew what we were really like, they wouldn't want anything to do with us. It focuses on all the things we're doing wrong or ways we're coming up short, or it repeatedly reminds us of past mistakes we've made or experiences we've had. Over time, we can end up feeling like there is something wrong with us, like we're broken. If this is an experience you've had, this chapter is for you. It's a different take on the idea of being broken and one that I hope will help you own your story—cracks, chips and all.

To start, let's talk about Japanese pottery (stay with me, this is relevant!). *Kintsukuroi* ("golden mend") is the Japanese art of mending broken pottery using lacquer resin laced with gold or silver.

As well as a nifty form of repair, *kintsukuroi* has a deeper philosophical significance. The mended flaws become part of the object's design. Some people believe the pottery to be even more beautiful, having been broken and repaired. Through *kintsukuroi*, the cracks and seams become a symbol of an event that happened in the object's life, rather than the cause of its destruction.

Like pots, bowls, cups, and plates, we endure our own bumps and scrapes. We experience dizzying drops from a previous high and unexpected knocks. Sometimes we experience things that plant the seeds of shame: rejection, betrayal, abandonment, failure. So we try to avoid situations that leave us vulnerable to these feelings as much as possible, lest the people around us see the evidence of how imperfect, flawed, and "not good enough" we are. We stay hidden in the cupboard, right behind the best silver, because we don't want to get a chip, a crack, or a complete break.

That's not to say that I believe trauma or tragedy automatically makes us more beautiful—I don't. As the saying goes, "Hurt people hurt people." I believe these experiences change us, though, and we have a choice. We can choose to reject our bitter experiences and flaws, to wish and will them away, or to regret, to pine, and to live in the land of "If only..." We can disguise with personas, cover up with defenses, distract with busy-ness. Or, we can choose to see these experiences for what they are: our golden seams.

The times when we get scratched, chipped, cracked, and broken can feel awful. But there can also be a strange beauty in the way we process them and the lessons we take from them afterwards—if we want. Our experiences don't define us, but they do influence us. We can decide to hide, or we can decide to embrace these experiences that have shaped us in some small way, the experiences to which we've applied our own special coating of gold-laced resin. We can decide to cover up, or we can decide to walk out into the world as ourselves, mended breaks and all.

This is the end of part one on feelings. We've looked at a range of common challenges related to our emotions, including how to be kind to ourselves we feel not good enough, and how to deal with fear, envy, overwhelm and other emotional experiences that are part of being human, but still hard. The next chapter kicks off part two, which is all about doing and the different ways we can respond to situations that might challenge our self-kindness as we live our days and get things done. We'll start by exploring how to be kind to ourselves when we (inevitably) make mistakes. Before that, though, take a minute to sit with this chapter and see what comes up.

Your moment of kindness:

Where are your golden seams?

What lessons have you learned from experiences you've had?

PART 2
DOING

TWELVE
HOW TO BE KIND TO YOURSELF WHEN YOU MAKE A MISTAKE

I did then what I knew how to do. Now that I know better, I do better.

—Maya Angelou

When I look at the many (many) mistakes I've made in my life, I can see they fall into two broad categories. First, there are the accidental-but-embarrassing moments, like having to run back to the airport gate just before they closed the cabin doors because I left my phone in the departure lounge then doing the walk of shame back down the cabin as the other passengers watched. There are also the mistakes that arise from conscious choices I've made. Mistakes like being short with my partner or kids when I'm feeling anxious or stressed about something else. Avoiding something important because it feels hard. Saying I'm going to do something, then neglecting to do it. Making a decision that prioritizes comfort over growth, and handling difficult situations in a way I don't feel good about later.

I find it challenging not to give myself a hard time about the choice-based mistakes I make, especially big ones that lead to negative consequences for other people. I have an internal voice that pipes up, "You know what else is like this? That thing you did seven years ago!" But, on good days, I can foster an appreciation for my mistakes; they help me learn more about who I want to become and how I want to deal with similar situations in the future.

What I've noticed about that voice above is it usually hooks into mistakes that are unresolved. Unthinking comments I made in the moment that I didn't revisit and address; errors of omission I never circled back and righted; things I avoided that I ended up sweeping under the rug rather than facing head-on—even with myself. Things that, years later, evoke a sinking sense of shame and reveal aspects of myself I find hard to accept. The things I address, right, and face? The energy behind them fades and they no longer provide ammunition for that voice.

We all make mistakes, big and small, but what matters is *how we respond to them*. No doubt you've experienced the spectrum of how other people respond to their mistakes, from justifying and avoiding to taking responsibility and making amends. You might remember how these different responses have landed when you're on the receiving end. You might know how it feels, and how the outcome shifts, when you're willing to take ownership of, and make amends for, mistakes. You probably also know how it feels and what happens when you don't.

Deep down, we know when we're doing the right thing, and when we're not. That knowledge often shows up first as a feeling somewhere in our bodies. A pit in our stomach, a tightness in our chest, a raising of our shoulders. Taking responsibility (or, as I shared in "How to Be Kind to

Yourself When "Self-Love" Feels Unrelatable," *response-ability*) might feel excruciating in the moment, but when it's done, it's done. Chances are, taking steps to rectify the situation will lift some of the heaviness surrounding it. And if we don't? I know when I continue to avoid, I carry that heaviness around, sometimes for years. The mistake lives with me, a loose end that snags every so often, reminding me of its presence and bringing the heaviness back.

The kindest thing we can do when we make a mistake—for ourselves and for other people—is to acknowledge what happened and make amends from a place of compassion. Here's the process that I've found helpful. I hope it's helpful to you, too.

Empathize with yourself

In my experience, this is the hardest but most important step. I used to worry that empathizing with myself was akin to letting myself off the hook. It's actually the opposite: empathizing isn't about shirking responsibility at all, it's about accepting reality. That can be as simple as saying "This happened" without attaching "because" or a story about how we're an awful person or someone else did something bad. Taking it a step further, we can then acknowledge "This happened and I feel… (embarrassed/hurt/ashamed/angry)."

Why does empathy matter? When I'm mired in shame and self-criticism, I'm far less likely to face up to what I've done and address it head-on. The nature of shame means we avoid the things we feel shame about. But when we shine empathy on the situation, shame can't survive. This might not happen the first time, the second or even the fifteenth. Shame can be pervasive and empathy hard to access, especially if we're dealing with a mistake that has triggered an old wound. Empathy isn't something we do once, and it's done, it's a practice. Like a language or a musical instrument, if we fall out of practice with empathy, it's going to take some time to refresh our skills.

For me, an important piece of empathy is acknowledging that no one or nothing else can make me respond a certain way. There can be certain situations, feelings, and behaviors that serve as triggers, but I have ownership of my response. It's not about blaming myself or other people, or (at the opposite end of the scale) condoning. Instead, it's taking a compassionate look at the complete picture and what I know to be true.

Whatever the mistake, we won't be able to move past it and make amends until we can empathize with why we did what we did. Something I find helpful when empathy feels out of reach is The Best Friend Test: "If my best friend came to me and told me about this situation, how would I respond?"

Examine what was happening underneath

We always have reasons for doing the things we do and saying the things we say, even if they aren't immediately obvious. Underneath every mistake, we can always find at least one reason or cause. This might be something as simple as a misunderstanding: we read the email in one tone, they read it in another. Perhaps we look within and realize we've been avoiding someone because they're going through a tough time; we're not sure what to say to them or don't want to say the wrong thing.

Sometimes we make mistakes that are rooted in deeper beliefs we have about ourselves. The good news is that once you're looking out for these beliefs, they are usually easy to recognize. The basic formula goes: "I did X, so I am Y." I said something without thinking, so I am unworthy of that person's friendship. I forgot to send that email, so I am disorganized, useless, and one day they're going to figure that out and replace me. I didn't meet that goal, so I am not good enough.

While we're not aware of these beliefs, they can become a self-fulfilling prophecy. We might not be a bad friend, but if we forget a friend's birthday then don't follow up because the "You forgot their birthday so you are a terrible friend and now they know how terrible you are" narrative is so uncomfortable we want to avoid it, then we end up behaving like a bad friend, whatever our intentions.

The kindest thing we can do for ourselves is to notice these belief-based internal soundtracks and switch them out for something more aligned with the person we want to be (and, on our good days, already are!) When I notice these kinds of thoughts popping up, I do two things to try to turn them around:

1. Looking for evidence to the contrary. "I am a terrible friend." Is that always true? Almost certainly not. So, when have I been a good friend? It's not usually enough to think about this evidence, so write it down. Our inner critic hijacks our internal thoughts, but reading external words on a page has a special power and positive effect. It's not just something we're trying to convince ourselves of by doing battle in our heads. The evidence is there on paper.

2. Asking "What would (the opposite) kind of person do in this situation?" Whatever my inner critic throws at me—I'm a terrible friend, I'm useless, I'm unworthy, etc. etc.—I can use as a starting point to flip it. I'm a terrible friend; what a *good friend* do in this situation?

I'm useless; what would a *useful person* do in this situation? I'm unworthy; how would a *worthy person* behave in this situation?

Not only does this kind of examination help us empathize with ourselves further, but it also provides us with the information we need to change this belief in the future. Once we're aware of the hidden beliefs that have driven our behavior in the past, we're far more likely to be aware of them in the future. This is as true, if not more so, for mistakes we seem to repeat, even though each time we tell ourselves things will be different from now on. In these situations, I'm reminded of the beautiful quote from the Buddhist Pema Chodron, "Nothing goes away until it teaches us what we need to know." Instead of beating ourselves up for making the same mistake repeatedly, curiosity and compassionate self-exploration become even more important. What do I still need to learn here? What would it look like to make a different choice next time?

Make amends

Apologizing when our mistakes affect someone else is important, but making amends (taking restitutive action) is even more so. This step is often the most challenging, which means it's also the most tempting to skip. But this is the step that will most affect how we feel about ourselves later on.

At the very least, your mistake will have affected you. It might have affected other people, too. Admitting our mistakes to ourselves can be hard enough, let alone admitting them to other people. To come back from a big mistake, however, we need to take steps toward making amends. As therapist Anne Katherine points out in her book *Where to Draw the Line*, making amends not only means apologizing. It also means taking action to show the people affected you want to make up for what happened. If I borrow a friend's dress and damage it beyond repair, apologizing would look like saying "I'm sorry." Making amends would look like offering to buy her a new dress. We can also make amends with ourselves, too, by taking steps to rectify the mistake or making a plan to minimize the chance of it happening again. Making amends doesn't mean the person (or persons) affected by our mistake has to forgive us. This process is as much about honoring our integrity and doing the right thing as it is about winning back favor with other people.

Get clear on what you're taking away

Just as there are usually reasons behind every mistake, there are also lessons you can take away from it. Although I don't love making mistakes, I find it easier to be kinder to myself in the face of bad choices or actions when I stop and look for the lesson. I used to think fixing mistakes was about going back to the way things were before, like pressing rewind on life and re-recording over the bits I'd rather forget. Viewing these situations through a lens of self-kindness and self-acceptance, though, I view mistakes in a different light. We are the sum of our experiences and how we respond to them. Mistakes are something we can grow through and come out the other side (hopefully) a little wiser and more self-aware. It's what the Urban Dictionary calls "AFGO" (Another F—ing Growth Opportunity). Painful, but an opportunity.

In the next chapter, we're exploring self-control, self-discipline, and how to approach these not-fun-but-necessary behaviors with self-kindness.

Your moment of kindness:

Think of a mistake you made recently and the story you told yourself about that mistake. What is the evidence that story is not the complete picture?

What would someone who was the opposite of the label in that story do?

If you haven't already done so, what is one step you can take to make amends for this mistake today?

THIRTEEN
HOW TO BE KIND TO YOURSELF WHEN IT FEELS LIKE YOU HAVE NO SELF-CONTROL

> You have power over your mind—not outside events. Realize this, and you will find strength.
>
> —Marcus Aurelius, Meditations

What do you think of when you hear the words "self-control"?

I think of the Stanford marshmallow experiment. In this study, researchers led a child into a room and sat them down. Then, they gave them a choice: they could have one treat now or wait while the tester left the room (without touching the original treat) and have two treats when they returned.

The testers were studying delayed gratification. When they did follow-up studies, they found the children who were willing and able to hold out for their two Oreos/marshmallows/pretzel sticks tended to have better SAT scores and academic achievement, lower BMI, and were judged by psychologist and study leader Walter Mischel to be "significantly more competent" than their peers who were less able to resist temptation. This study has since become a go-to demonstration of why self-control is important; it correlates with positive outcomes in many areas of life.

The factors that affect self-control in the real world

But this study is also only a 2D view of how self-control works in the real world. In the original study, testers began by showing the children they could trust them. Before the true experiment began, the children already believed if the tester would do what they said. If they said they would be back in 15 minutes with two marshmallows, they would be.

In real life, the outcomes of delayed gratification are often not so clear-cut or reliable. More often than not, we're required to delay gratification for something that might or might not happen within an unspecified amount of time. We might have grown up in an environment where promises and commitments weren't honored. This would also affect our sense of what researchers referred to as "environmental reliability." Spending our lives waiting for a marshmallow that won't arrive (or we don't believe will) isn't a sign of competence or rational decision-making. In fact, it's arguably the opposite.

My biggest issue with how we talk about this study (and self-control), is the suggestion that self-control is something we either have or don't, and something set from childhood. As other studies have suggested, self-control and willpower are finite resources. A multitude of factors influence them, from our environment, to how we're feeling, to the time of day.

Most of all, many of the conventional discussions about self-control make it sound like a drag. It's something we all know we should have, but it's something most of us struggle with in certain situations. There's no denying self-control is a useful muscle to exercise. But having negative associations with it means we're more likely to avoid facing it head-on, rather than finding creative and compassionate ways to mediate with ourselves.

An alternative view of self-control

Another study by Alexander Soutschek at the University of Zurich offers a fresh perspective on self-control. This version is less about discipline and more about self-kindness. It suggests our level of self-control is influenced by the same region of the brain that is associated with prosocial behavior, such as overcoming our own perspective to experience empathy for others.

As the theory goes, empathy is about being able to see things from someone else's position and perspective, to walk a mile in their shoes. With self-control, we show empathy, but for ourselves—specifically, our future selves. Our future selves are almost like a different person. They have had experiences we haven't had yet; they are living in a world different to ours. We can only imagine what they are like and what life is like for them. Self-control is about forgoing something in the present to benefit our future selves.

I like this way of looking at self-control because it removes the heaviness and angst. We are motivated by wanting the best for ourselves, rather than wanting to avoid the negative consequences of failing in life. This difference in motivation is subtle, but important.

When I think about self-control as empathy for my future self, it feels like a much more attractive prospect. Self-control transforms from something I know I "should" do to something that fits my values of empathy, compassion, and self-kindness.

Turning this insight into action

So what does having self-control motivated by empathy for our future selves look like in practice? Here are three practices I've been using to redefine my relationship with the term "self-control" and make better decisions:

1. Put yourself in your future self's shoes:

A useful exercise when we're struggling with self-kindness and compassion is to think, "How would I respond if I were talking to my best friend about this?" We can also use this with self-control. A question I love is *"What can I do today that my future self would thank me for?"*

2. Imagine your future self as another person:

Visualize "Future You" as a different person, with different situations, challenges and feelings. They are living in a different context (i.e. the future). Seeing them as a separate person (and the distance and perspective this provides) makes it easier to empathize with that version of ourselves and also reminds us that there is more than just the here and now. Future Me has to live with the consequences of the decisions of past and present me, and the same goes for Future You.

3. Ask your future self for advice:

The final empathy-related practice is a combination of the previous two. We're visualizing our future selves as a separate person but we're also considering their perspective by asking them, "What advice do you have for me in this situation?" or "What do you think I should do right now?" Without a crystal ball, our answers to these questions will be educated guesses, but that's OK. The more we can practice visualizing our future self responding to this question, the more likely we are to empathize with that version of ourselves in the present.

Your moment of kindness:

How does thinking about self-control as empathy for your future self change how you feel about it?

What can you do today that your future self will thank you for?

FOURTEEN
HOW TO BE KIND TO YOURSELF WHEN YOU'RE LACKING CONFIDENCE

> People are like stained-glass windows. They sparkle and shine when the sun is out, but when the darkness sets in their true beauty is revealed only if there is light from within.
>
> —Elisabeth Kübler-Ross

I started my personal growth journey in therapy. When I first walked into the therapist's office, I was struggling with confidence. In my mind, I would walk out again 3-6 months later with a state of unflappable inner peace and certainty.

I soon learned this is a myth. Yes, there are plenty of gurus and self-described enlightened people who might say this kind of inner Zen is what we should strive for (Never feeling anger! Zero judgment of other people! Detachment from everything!). But let's be real: we're people, not robots.

I'm happier when I acknowledge that, at times, I struggle. I have those "Who am I to be doing this?" thoughts, and days where I doubt myself and what I'm doing. I get vulnerability hangovers. I like to be in control (and will give the side-eye to anyone who says uncertainty is a necessary part of life, even though I know they're right—sigh.).

And I've learned I can have these experiences and still experience confidence, and that's called being human. At any point, we're all sitting somewhere on the confidence continuum.

Confidence is a process and a work in progress, not a permanent state of being

I used to think of confidence as being like a light switch. With the right formula and the right ingredients, I could flick that switch to "on" and never have to worry about struggling with confidence again. But confidence is something we nurture. Although there are plenty of things we can do to enhance the level of confidence we experience in our lives, it ebbs and flows for all of us.

Expecting ourselves to feel 100% confidence all the time becomes a vicious cycle, because when we struggle with confidence, we doubt ourselves even more. Instead, think of confidence as being like a series of waves. We get to influence how big the peaks and troughs become, but it is natural for our confidence to ebb and flow.

Confidence comes from action (not the other way around)

If I had a pound for every time I've told myself "I want to do X, but I need to feel more confident first," I would be writing this from my luxury cat sanctuary in Bora Bora (or still waiting until I felt confident enough to set it up).

Like motivation, confidence comes *from* action, not the other way around. The idea that we need to feel confident before we can do that thing we really want to do is a clever justification for staying comfortable and avoiding the hard feelings that come with stepping outside what's familiar. The first step is to try something, anything; avoidance will suck any confidence we have dry. It's easy to overthink this step, to want to make sure we're focusing on the "right" action, and to get stuck in analysis paralysis, second-guessing ourselves without ever actually doing anything. But this stage is really about experimentation. Take the pressure off, give yourself a free pass to choose the "wrong" action, and just do *something*.

The reason taking action on something—anything—is important is because it brings us to the next step, which is clarity. Clarity comes when we get feedback from our actions. That feedback might be, "Hey, that wasn't so bad after all. Maybe I'm on to something here!" It might also be, "Oops, guess that didn't go so well…"

Whatever the outcome is, your action will lead you to a sense of what's right for you and what's not right for you, what works and what doesn't. The more you try, the more clarity you will get, and the deeper your confidence will become.

Focus on the very next step

We don't need to know *how* we're going to do something in order to feel confident, but we need to know *what* we're going to do. Confidence doesn't come from certainty we can do something with grace and dignity 100% of the time. Like I mentioned above, it comes from knowing what we need to try next.

When we're embarking on a new and/or big project, change, or other life adventure, the chances are we don't have all the answers about how it will work from day one. The experience of working on most big projects is like walking down a path in a heavy mist. You can see a couple of steps in front of you, but the rest of the path remains hidden. As you take those two steps, the next couple of steps reveal themselves, then the next, and so on. This uncertainty, of not being able to see more than a couple of steps ahead, can leave us feeling like we're not ready, which in turn can leave us feeling like we just shouldn't do that thing. After all, it's better to wait until we feel ready, right? As you might remember from the section above, this line of thinking is a tricky trick our minds play on us to keep us well within our comfort zones. Remember (stick it to your fridge, make it your screensaver, order it as a temporary tattoo), *confidence comes from action, not the other way around.*

In this context, that means it's OK if you don't know what the "how" looks like right now. The only thing that matters is: what is the very next action you need to take?

One foot in front of the other, one step at a time.

Arrogance is the opposite of confidence

Arrogance often masquerades as confidence, but it's a thin shell of inflated self-importance hiding deep-rooted insecurities underneath. Confidence is rooted in growth toward and belief in our capability to be the best version of ourselves. Arrogance is rooted in avoiding uncomfortable feelings and truths about ourselves.

When we work with the basic belief that confident person = good person, unconfident person = bad person, we're a lot more likely to "Fake it 'til we make it," to borrow a popular saying. "Making it," in this context, involves convincing other people we're confident, regardless of how we actually feel deep down. As psychologist and author Amy Cuddy says in her TED talk, 'Your Body Language May Shape Who You Are," a better alternative is "Fake it 'til we *become* it." Arrogance is rooted in appearances and power plays; confidence is rooted in how we feel about ourselves.

If you're worried about appearing arrogant, chances are you're fine, because people who are genuinely arrogant don't worry about it! True confidence involves acknowledging we don't always feel confident, that we're not always right or the best, and feeling at peace with that. When we are confident, we have nothing to prove because knowing that for ourselves is enough.

Struggling with confidence isn't a reflection of your abilities

A lack of confidence isn't evidence that we're not capable of doing something. Correlation doesn't equal causation. A reminder I find helpful is "Just because I think something negative about myself doesn't mean it's automatically true." While it is the case that sometimes a lack of confidence can be an indicator we need to brush up on our skills or experience, more often than not, there's something (or things) else affecting how we feel. Our self-concept, experiences we've had in the past, childhood messages, our evolutionary wiring (thanks, lizard brain), our feelings of worthiness and deserving... all of those things can present as "I can't do this," but that's not reality. Our levels of confidence aren't necessarily reflective of our abilities, which is why it's also important to look for the evidence we can do the task at hand.

One way to tell if your confidence is rooted in reality or fear is to look for "When... then..." thinking (for example, "When I've done X, then I'll be ready"). First, ask yourself, "Is it true I need to do/have/experience whatever X is before I can start?" (90% of the time, the answer is no). Also, look for the criteria changing. Once you complete X, is it immediately replaced by Y? If so, this might be a sign that you're being hijacked by a lack of confidence, not a lack of ability. You can also look to the past for this evidence. If you've done something similar in the past, what worked for you then? Even if you're trying something you've never attempted before and stretching yourself way outside of your comfort zone, rather than focus on the reasons you can't do this, might fail, or might fall short, think about times when you've risen to the challenge before. When you've tried new and untested things in other areas of life, what happened? If the outcome was positive, what made it so? And if not, what could you do differently this time?

This kind of questioning helps counter the stories and fears of our inner critics with evidence that is a fairer reflection of reality. It takes practice to question these thoughts, but the more you can do it, even after the fact, the more natural it will become.

Expect it to be hard (but doable)

When we're tackling new challenges that take us outside our comfort zone, most of us assume, even unconsciously, that at some point, things will become easy. Our confidence will become unshakable because we know we can do this and nothing can stop us. Challenges? Pah! What challenges?

In reality, as author Melodie Beattie describes in her book *Stop Being Mean to Yourself,* life is like a video game. We conquer one set of challenges and we level up. A new level of a game isn't easier: in fact, it gets harder. We have to use everything we've learned so far *and* add new skills into the mix, too. We face a new set of challenges, and, with those challenges, a new set of opportunities for a richer, bolder, more authentic life. Entrepreneur, coach, and speaker Ishita Gupta used the phrase "New level, new devil" to illustrate this idea when I interviewed her a few years ago. She reiterated the idea that things don't get easier. We just face different flavors of challenges as we move onwards and upwards.

It's true that if we tell ourselves something will be hard, we're more likely to focus on the parts that are hard and ignore the things that go well. However, if we expect things to get easier and they don't, we can be left wondering what's wrong with us and whether we're cut out for whatever it is we're doing. The approach I've found most helpful when trying something new or stretching myself (and feeling decidedly unconfident) is to expect it to be hard, but doable. Whatever path you're on is unlikely to get easier or more comfortable, but that's part of the process. Far from being a sign there's something wrong with us, it's a sign we're growing and evolving.

There is more than one way to deepen your confidence

Lots of people suggest techniques like affirmations, journaling, coaching, therapy, standing naked in front of the mirror, and so on. If those things work for you, that's great. Keep going.

But there is no one-size-fits-all approach to confidence. If you try to apply practices that feel un-genuine or inauthentic, don't experience the promised benefits, and tell yourself you must be doing it wrong (or worse, that there's something wrong with you since they seem to work for so many people), this won't help your feelings of confidence. For me, saying affirmations and mirror self-talk are two of those things. They feel ridiculous, so I don't do them. Luckily, there are other ways to explore and deepen my feelings around confidence, including journaling, guided meditation, and more. Those things might feel ridiculous to the mirror talkers, and that's OK, too. Remember what we said about comparisons? What works for other people doesn't matter as much as what works for us. A key component of true confidence is being able to choose your right path, even when it might be different from the path other people are taking. And that starts right now. In the next chapter, we'll be building on the ideas here and talking about self-kindness and goals. In the meantime, take a few moments to reflect on what came up for you during this chapter.

Your moment of kindness:

Where could you use an extra confidence boost in your life right now?

What is one action you can take toward that today?

FIFTEEN
HOW TO BE KIND TO YOURSELF WHEN YOU'RE SETTING BIG GOALS

If you don't know where you are going, you will probably end up somewhere else.

—Lawrence J. Peter, *Peter's Quotations: Ideas for Our Time*

At the end of each year, one of my favorite rituals is to think about goals for the new year. Even though it's an arbitrary point in our calendar, there is still something exciting about the possibilities the next 365 days might hold.

Now, I love goals, but I know not everyone shares this love. If goals aren't your thing and you're tempted to skim-read this chapter, that's A-OK. You do what works for you. But goals don't have to be (and shouldn't be) stressful, pressured, insecurity-inducing sources of tension in our lives. If they are, and that's why you shy away from creating them for yourself, this chapter is for you (also, not wanting to set goals for yourself? That's a goal. Just saying...).

The taller a tree grows, the deeper its roots need to be. The higher the building, the lower the foundations. As we dive into how to approach goal-setting with self-kindness, I want to start with the principles—the roots and foundations—of setting feel-good goals.

1. Feel-good goals start with asking "What do I really want?"

One of the most common goal-setting mistakes is that we commit to goals we think we should work toward without stopping to ask what we want, or what's best for us right now. We compare ourselves to other people, experience FOMO (the fear of missing out; we talk about this more in my chapter on How to Be Kind to Yourself When You're Experiencing FOMO) or want validation from a certain person or group of people. All these things can influence our goals in subtle (and not so subtle) ways.

With every decision we make, our motivations fall into one of two categories: intrinsic and extrinsic. Intrinsic motivations include those which are to do with our fulfillment, integrity, and growth. Extrinsic motivations relate to what we think we should do, external validation, or how we think other people will perceive us. We might want to impress or please other people, try to control what they think of us, or avoid conflict.

With any goal, it's natural to have a mix of intrinsic and extrinsic motivations, but we want to make sure the former outweigh the latter. It's much easier to stick to goals that are rooted in intrinsic motivation, especially when the going gets tough, and you'll be much happier and more fulfilled in the process.

If you're not sure whether a goal is intrinsically or extrinsically motivated, sit down and make a list of all the reasons you want to achieve that goal. Be honest—brutally honest—with yourself and try to refrain from judgment or conclusions right now. If one reason is, "I want to show my ex that I'm doing great," or, "I want my mother's approval," add that to the list—no shame. Discovering that you are pursuing a goal to impress someone else isn't a reason to ditch it. But you'll need to find more intrinsic motivations to sustain you in the long term. Get conscious of all the reasons you want to do what you're doing and focus on the aspects that align with your personal values and needs.

2. Feel-good goals sometimes look more like challenges than goals

When I am excited about a goal, I become over-optimistic about how much I will achieve in a short space of time, and underestimate how challenging it might be. The result is that, unless I catch myself, I set unreachable milestones. Then, I fall behind, and start feeling guilty and annoyed that I'm not sticking to my original plan. Eventually, I give up, feeling demoralized and like I'm not cut out to do whatever it is I want to do.

Something that has helped break this cycle is gamification. Gamification comes in many forms, from private challenges we keep to ourselves, to group events involving public declarations and large communities. When I wanted to read more, I set myself an annual reading challenge with different genres of books. When I wanted to write a novel, but found that every attempt petered out, I tried

National Novel Writing Month (an annual challenge where participants aim to write 50,000 words in a month). These kinds of group challenges can be helpful for tackling big projects that can feel slow and solitary otherwise. You also can try setting yourself 30, 60 or 90-day challenges, or aiming for longer and longer "streaks" and beating your personal best. The more you look for it, the more you'll see gamification popping up everywhere, from habit apps, to language-learning, and even journaling. This is because it works. The style of gamification doesn't matter so much as the challenge feeling fun, exciting, and inspiring.

3. Feel-Good goals support each other

We all have a set of human needs. They range from basic things like water, food and oxygen, to more complex desires, like growth and personal fulfillment. Between those two points is a wide spectrum and, within that spectrum, we want to make sure that we're not meeting one need at the expense of another.

Quitting your job and going to live on the beach in Thailand might meet your need for adventure. If you also have a strong need for stability and security, though, there might be aspects of this set-up that won't work so well for you. Equally, impulse-buying that pair of designer boots might satisfy your need for spontaneity and excitement. If you use your adult-education fund to buy them, however, then it's going to be at the expense of your need for growth and learning.

There might very well be a time and place for moving to Thailand or designer booties, but feel-good goals consider all our needs, not just the inner voice that's in the driving seat at the moment of decision.

4. Feel-Good Goals focus on seeking growth, rather than avoiding pain

At a basic level, our goals are driven by one of two things: avoiding pain or seeking growth. Both can be highly motivating to start with, but when we pursue goals based on the former, we are more likely to enter a frustrating start-stop cycle that leaves us feeling like we're not getting anywhere.

Let's take exercise as an example. In the past, I would make a renewed vow to exercise consistently whenever I noticed my jeans were feeling a little too tight (pain). Once I was happier with my appearance (pain avoided), I stopped, only for the entire cycle to begin again. Now, I exercise because I feel better when I do and because I enjoy setting myself physical challenges (growth). Rather than being a way of avoiding pain and assuaging discomfort, it's become something that encourages me to challenge myself and enjoy.

If you notice choices and behavior that are motivated by wanting to avoid pain, ask yourself: "What would seeking growth look like?" You might not know immediately, and that's fine. Stay curious, keep noticing, keep questioning, and the answers will appear.

5. Feel-Good Goals focus on the process (and what you can control)

You might have already come across the concept of SMART goals. SMART stands for a series of criteria: Specific, Measurable, Actionable (or Attractive), Realistic, and Timed. While these criteria are useful to think about, there is one crucial ingredient that is missing: we have to enjoy (or at least find meaning) in the *process* of reaching that goal. If we get too fixated on the goal itself, we end up living in the future, chasing something that doesn't yet exist. We also become obsessed with an outcome and miss out on something very important: the here and now. Another reason why focusing on the process is important is that we rarely have full control over whether we achieve our goals. For example, "I want to find love this year" is a meaningful goal, but you are only 50% of that equation. It requires someone to love you in return, which isn't something you have power over. Things you can control include how many dates you go on, how you show up in your relationships, how many extra-curricular activities you get involved in, how much you work on your own sense of self, and so on. But the result? Unfortunately, that's not something any of us have control over. The same applies to many other kinds of goals: run a marathon, move house, have a baby, get into college, get a promotion... We can't guarantee any of these outcomes. What we can control: how we show up and do our bit.

The other way we can upset this balance is by giving too much control away through waiting to be found, rescued, or discovered. For example, if you want to start your own website, blog, or online project, taking the "If I build it they will come" mentality, setting up a blog and expecting people to find and flock to your fledgling website won't work. Instead, you need to make it as easy as possible for people to find you and pursue opportunities to get your writing/photography/whatever it is you're creating in front of more eyes. This approach is much more uncomfortable, but you're also much more likely to see the results you want from it. As author James Altucher explains in his eponymous book, instead of waiting for someone to discover you and choose you, "choose yourself."

To create goals based on self-kindness, we need to fall in love with the process. Reaching a particular goal is fantastic, but it's a temporary state. Soon, we find the goalposts shift. Now that our original goal has stopped being a goal and become the norm, we're out chasing the next big dream. The goal itself is temporary and fleeting. The process, on the other hand, is life. The process is what we are living day in, day out as we move closer to a life that's aligned with our values, needs, and preferences. It's what we experience as we stretch ourselves to grow and as we expand our sense of what's possible. By focusing on the process, we might or might not meet our goals, but we'll still get a lot out of trying.

So, you've set your big goals (and done so from a place of self-kindness). Now, the real work begins. The next chapter is all about motivation—something we think we need, but (spoiler alert!) we don't. If you have a tricky relationship with motivation, this one is for you. For now, though, it's time to review the ideas that resonated with you from this chapter and put them into practice.

Your moment of kindness:

Think of a goal you're currently working toward and run it through the framework above. Are there any changes you can make to how you're approaching your goal that would make it more feel-good?

SIXTEEN
HOW TO BE KIND TO YOURSELF WHEN YOU'RE FINDING IT HARD TO GET MOTIVATED

When you're trying to motivate yourself, appreciate the fact that you're even thinking about making a change.

—Alice Domar, PhD

Motivation can feel like a mythical beast, appearing and vanishing without warning. In my work as a creative coach, one of the biggest obstacles writing clients used to talk about was a lack of motivation. It came up in many contexts, but the scenario was all too relatable: *I want to write/create/do this thing, but I'm struggling to find the motivation to act on it.*

This is something I've also grappled with. Whenever I think or say "I want to do X, I just don't feel motivated," there's one of two things going on:

1) Deep down, I *don't* want to do X. I think I should. Other people seem to be doing it, and I feel pressure to do it. But, hand on heart, it's not a good fit, it doesn't align with my values, and/or I don't truly want to.

2) It's not about motivation. What appears as a lack of motivation can mask something deeper. This might be fear, of failure, of success, or of change. It might be uncertainty about whether this endeavor will work out. It might be vulnerability, anxiety around judgment, and that small voice that says "But what will people think of me?" Maybe the thing we want to do puts us way outside our comfort zone, and a lack of motivation is an effective way to avoid facing that discomfort.

Motivation alone is rarely the issue, which means it's also not the panacea for all our problems. So how can we approach struggles with motivation from a place of self-kindness? This chapter is all about dealing with motivation and resistance with self-compassion.

Make friends with your resistance

Like most people, I experience resistance daily. Exercise; writing; answering emails; putting plates straight into the dishwasher instead of leaving them on the side... If I do it on a semi-regular basis, inevitably I experience *the resistance*.

Look under the hood, and most of the time, you'll find resistance is a conflict between long-term benefit and short-term comfort. Much of what we do in the interests of long-term benefit doesn't feel that nice, fun, or even comfortable in the short term. Exercise is a great example of this. If we do it enough, we can get to a place where we enjoy it. If we're out of shape, however, there's an adjustment period where it feels uncomfortable (even tortuous). The thing is, we need to go through that to get before we can get to the good feelings.

The solution to resistance is not to stop feeling it, it's learning how to listen and respond to it. Resistance is 100% human, and it's something everyone experiences (the author Steven Pressfield wrote an excellent book about this called *The War of Art*).

Resistance can also be helpful; sometimes, it contains a message. I've experienced resistance when doing something that doesn't fit my values or isn't right for me. I've also experienced resistance when I'm facing something that would require me to step out of my comfort zone and grow.

In both cases, resistance is an opportunity for greater personal awareness and growth. Get to know your personal flavor of resistance. Notice what it feels like physically to experience resistance. What thoughts go through your head when you experience resistance? Pay attention to the situations you're in when you notice resistance surfacing. Through listening out for our resistance, we can learn to tell the difference between "integrity alert" resistance and "growth opportunity" resistance.

Here are some questions to ask yourself as you explore this. If resistance is something you've been grappling with in your own life, I invite you to explore these questions through writing.

1. Will this thing that I'm feeling resistance toward bring me closer to, or take me further away from, my values and goals?

2. What influences my resistance? What patterns do I notice around when it comes up? (For example, does it mostly show up when I'm tired, hungry, or stressed?)

3. What are the beliefs behind the resistance? Am I coming from a place of "not enough" or a place of self-care?

4. What will my life be like three months, six months, a year from now if I start doing this thing today?

5. What will my future self most thank me for?

... And then move past it

Making friends with our resistance doesn't mean basking in it. The emotional experience of resistance and procrastination is often much worse than just doing the thing we're resisting. Instead, it's about taking action based on what we've learned about ourselves and using that learning to shift our perspective and change our behavior.

Remember that action precedes motivation

The idea we need to feel motivated to do something is a common misperception. Yes, motivation makes taking action easier and more comfortable, but it's not required. In reality, it works the other way around. The more we take action, the more motivated we'll feel to take action, and the stronger this virtuous circle will become.

Begin with the idea that you are in control and forget most of what you've been taught about motivation. Motivation can feel like a powerful, omnipotent force, but it's just a feeling. And we are more than our feelings. Whatever you want to do, it's within your power to do that—motivation or no motivation.

Think of the magic money jar

A few years ago, I interviewed endurance athlete Nicole Antoinette. During our conversation, she shared the wonderful analogy of the magic money jar.

Imagine someone gave you a money jar at the start of the year. This jar had magical properties and, if you tapped it once each day, a dollar would appear in the jar. There were rules attached to the magic. You could only get a maximum of one dollar a day, however many times you tapped, and if you missed a day, you couldn't catch up. No tap, no dollar. The first couple of months, things go well. You tap each day and it's fun to watch your magic money grow! But then something happens—an emergency crops up, you go away for a while, and in your haste you forget to bring the jar with you. When you come back, two weeks have passed without a single tap and you have no way to catch up on those missed dollars.

At this point, you have a choice: do you tell yourself, "Oh well, I skipped two weeks so I guess there's not much point in tapping again now." Or, do you say: "OK, I missed two weeks but if I start tapping again now, I'll still have $350 by the end of the year."

In this scenario, it's an easy decision: we would all opt for the latter and keep our daily dollars rolling in. But, as Nicole pointed out, we approach most of our habits and goals with the former mindset. We fall off the wagon and use that fact as a reason to stay there.

The next time you notice your important habits slipping or stray from the path of your meaningful goals, say to yourself, "Magic money jar!" and give it another tap.

Ask yourself: "Who do I need to become to do this?"

When we start a new project or habit, we usually focus on what we need to *do* to make that habit or project happen. A more important question is "Who do I need to *become* to do this?" I find this question useful as it shifts my focus away from whether I feel motivated toward the qualities I need to embody. Although it's a small shift in awareness, it's enough to help me think about the situation differently. As a bonus, it also helps me connect with my intrinsic motivation, since the person I need to become is usually aligned with the person I want to be, anyway.

Imagine yourself a year from now living a life where your goals and/or resolutions have come to fruition. How does that version of yourself behave? What kinds of thoughts do they have? What changes have they made in other areas of their lives? Who do they hang out with? What are they passionate about? Imagine that version of yourself and, most importantly, connect with how they *feel*. This can help kick your motivation into gear and get you started toward making this vision a reality.

Practice the 20-Second Rule

For every behavior or habit we want to add to our lives, it can help to identify a behavior or habit to replace (ahem, mindless Facebook scrolling). In *The Happiness Advantage*, Shawn Achor describes what he calls the 20-Second Rule. This involves creating an environment where it takes us 20 seconds longer to do the thing we want to stop doing, and easier to do the replacement habit or activity instead.

For example, if you want to read more after work but you find yourself enveloped in the warm embrace of Netflix each night instead, change your set-up. Put a book on the sofa in place of your tablet or laptop before you leave for work in the morning. If necessary, unplug your TV. It's easy to plug it back in, but it takes extra time, and this can be enough to remind you what you'd rather be doing instead. When I wanted to spend less time aimlessly browsing social media, I moved the apps to the third page of my home screen. I also moved all the apps I wanted to use (reading, journaling and learning Spanish) to the first page instead. Whenever I opened my phone, these apps were now the first thing I saw. Even if my intention was to check Facebook or Instagram, I would see these app icons and remember my pledge to read more books, learn a language, and maintain a regular journaling practice. It's not a failsafe change, but it helps.

Respect your energy patterns

When I'm planning my upcoming week, I make two lists. One list contains tasks and activities for when my energy is at its highest (i.e. those that need brain power and creative juice). The other contains brainless tasks that are perfect for low-energy periods.

I used to expect myself to be "on" all day, while also getting frustrated that I wasn't. Since learning that everyone's energy undulates throughout the day, I've found it helpful to track when my energy is highest and lowest. I've also become more aware of things that have a positive or negative influence on my energy levels (certain types of foods, how much sleep I get, and so on). The face is, we don't—and can't—function at 100% all day. Accepting there will be low-energy times (and tracking when these are) helps us work with ourselves and our natural rhythms.

One of the most helpful books on energy and productivity I've read is *The Way We're Working Isn't Working* by Tony Schwartz. He shares more helpful information about tuning into your energy patterns. If this concept resonates with you, I recommend taking a closer look at his work.

Start with 10 minutes

When I worked with writers who were struggling with motivation, this was usually where we would start. Some clients would come to coaching having tried to work for two hours on their book every day. They would stop after a short while because the realities of what it takes to do two hours daily set in (it takes a lot), and their motivation plummeted to zero. Other clients had trouble getting started and felt lost in a fog of analysis paralysis that left them feeling demotivated and hopeless. The simple but surprisingly effective antidote to these, and other motivation-related issues, is to start with 10 minutes.

More often than not, once we start whatever it is we're trying to do (because starting is usually the hardest part of the process), we want to carry on for longer. But—and this is an important part of this rule—if you don't want to carry on for longer than 10 minutes, you have permission to stop. Tomorrow is another day and, while 10 minutes might not be long enough to move mountains, it adds up to progress over time. Anything is better than nothing.

As I mentioned above, action precedes motivation, and this is why the 10-minute rule is helpful. Doing something for 10 minutes, even if we're not feeling motivated, feels achievable. Doing something for two hours in the same situation? You can bet our inner procrastinators are going to have a field day with that. 10 minutes also feels doable when we're not sure exactly what we're doing. It's long enough to try something, but not so long that we end up feeling overwhelmed with all the things we don't know yet.

Find the simplest, most basic step you can take today and take it. You don't need to wait until your fears, anxieties, and avoidance have subsided. You can feel fear, accept your fear, and still take action. You can notice you're worried about what other people might think, and you can still take action. You can observe your desire to avoid discomfort, and you can still decide to face that avoidance head-on.

Remember, you already have everything you need to get started; it's just about doing it. Once you've taken that first step, you'll know you can take the next step, the next, and the next after that. And each step will bring you closer to where you want to be and who you want to become.

Your moment of kindness:

Where are you struggling with motivation right now?

Which of the practices above feels like it would be most helpful? Choose one and try it today.

SEVENTEEN
HOW TO BE KIND TO YOURSELF WHEN YOU'RE TOO BUSY FOR SELF-CARE

The one thing you can control is how you treat yourself. And that one thing can change everything.

—Leeana Tankersley

Self-kindness isn't a destination at which we arrive, it's a daily practice. But it's one that often falls by the wayside. Many of us feel like we don't have the time or the energy to carve out deliberate time for self-kindness and self-care. After all, there are far more important things we need to get done. This is especially true for people who have kids, a demanding job, financial pressures, others to care for, health problems, or similar commitments. Self-care is healthcare. It's not a luxury, it's a necessity—especially when we are taking care of tiny humans or have other big responsibilities. In this chapter, I'm going to show you how "I don't have time" doesn't always need to be the whole story. I'm going to invite you to question whether it is a lack of time or energy getting in the way, or something else. I'm also going to share a couple of self-kindness practices that take five minutes or less for those busy days when you are stretched to the max.

You *might* have time?

I don't know you, and I don't know your life, so I won't tell you that, of course, you have time and you're making excuses. There is a possibility you don't (in which the chapter "How to Be Kind to Yourself When You're Feeling Overwhelmed" might be helpful).

I'm also aware we tell ourselves stories and make statements like this that aren't entirely true. I would be remiss if I didn't acknowledge and explore that, too. Sometimes "I don't have time" is a justification masking something else—a belief, a fear, an internal story—rather than a valid reason. With things we truly want to do (or think we should do), we make time for them. Think back to the last time you did this with something that mattered to you. This is proof you can manage your own time— chances are, you're better at doing so than you realize. Having enough time is often not the whole issue. We can make time, but it can feel harder to do so when that time is for ourselves.

Self-kindness involves being upfront with ourselves. Honesty isn't one of the practices I'm going to discuss in this chapter, but it is a foundational act of self-kindness. If you've used time as a reason not to engage in self-care, start being honest with yourself. Instead of "I don't have time," "I have a busy schedule" or "I have too many other things going on," this might look like:

I'm not doing this because I love the idea of self-care but it feels selfish.

I'm not doing this because part of me believes self-care sounds ridiculous.

I'm not doing this because I have set ideas about how long I "should" spend on self-care and I don't have that kind of time.

I'm not doing this because it feels uncomfortable to say no to other people so I can spend time on myself.

I'm not doing this because I don't feel like I deserve it.

Your reasons will be personal to you but, by peeling back the layers and exploring your resistance, you'll understand yourself better and begin to shift these underlying beliefs.

When people call me on my justifications, I'm usually tempted to retreat, explaining "Well, that's easy for you to say..." And to some extent it is: like I said above, I know nothing about your life or what you're dealing with right now. But I would still like you to consider that you *could* make time for this. Yes, self-care has become yet another buzzword most of us are tired of hearing about. But another way of thinking about this is: do you have time to get sick? What about *really* sick? Do you have time to burn out? Do you have time to be functioning at 50% of your capacity? You and your wellbeing are important. Especially if you have kids; especially if you have a demanding job; especially if you have other people to take care of; especially if you have health issues. You're in a much better position to deal with all those things when you make time for yourself.

Get back to basics

When our plates are overflowing with competing commitments and demands, it's easy to get mired in the minutiae of individual tasks and commitments. If you're feeling overwhelmed and struggling to figure out what's important, try prioritizing using broader categories. For example:

1. Health
2. Relationships
3. Work

Even if this looks too simplistic, try it. When deciding on our priorities, the simpler and easier to act on, the better.

When honing in on your priorities, remember that to give, you need to have something to give. A common analogy for self-care is that of filling our cups. During busy times or when we're feeling overwhelmed and stressed, our cups can run dry. So we want them to be overflowing. That way, we can give to our commitments without draining ourselves. The only way we can do that is by placing our basic needs high on our priority list. It sounds, and feels, counterintuitive. It often brings us back to that resistance: isn't it self-indulgent to spend time on myself when there is so much else going on? But it's a basic law of physics: energy cannot be created or destroyed, it can only be changed. If you're changing personal energy into activity, you also need to draw on other kinds of energy to recharge your personal stores.

When we have this list clear in our minds, we also reduce the amount of decision fatigue we experience. We know, for example, our health gets our attention first, our relationships come next, then work comes after that. With this kind of hierarchy, it's much easier to plan our days and decide about how to spend any moments in our day we can eke out. The order of our top priorities might change in the short term, depending on what's happening in different areas of our lives. There might be times we want to make relationships number one or times when we want to devote more attention to a work project for a week. Even then, it helps to be aware of the status quo and to make conscious adjustments, rather than sailing through life without a compass.

7 Quick Self-Care Suggestions You Can Do at Any time

Since I became a mother, my amount of time for anything is approximately 1/100000th of what it was before. I'd heard people say, "I don't know what I used to do with all my time before I had kids," and used to think "Really? I have plenty to do." Now? I get it; I have no idea what I used to do with my time before I had kids.

I love my kids; I love spending time with them, and I'm grateful to spend most of each day with them. They are awesome! At the same time, I also like writing, I enjoy making things; I need to exercise, and I like self-care (showering is in there somewhere too). And I don't just like these things, they are expressions of core needs for me: creativity, movement and self-connection (not to mention cleanliness).

If you're in a similar position to me, whether that's because you are a parent, have a demanding job, other commitments, or are simply busy, I want to share a few quick self-care suggestions you can do almost anywhere, anytime, no matter what else is happening in life. If you'd like even more ideas for self-care, I invite you to check out my book, *From Coping to Thriving: How to Turn Self-Care Into a Way of Life*, which guides you through how to turn self-care into a way of life and contains dozens of practical suggestions. For now, here are a few to get you started:

1: H.A.L.T.

H.A.L.T. Stands for Hungry, Angry, Lonely, Tired and is a way of checking in with ourselves about whether our basic human needs are met. Because these needs are foundational, they can have an astonishing impact on how we feel. They are also all simple to fulfill. I find this exercise especially useful if I'm experiencing a general sense of malaise or unease. It's all too easy for me to become stuck in my head, trying to brainstorm answers about why I'm feeling this way. The answer might simply be, "I need to drink a glass of water," or "I didn't sleep well last night."

2: Mini-retreat

A mini-retreat is something you can do from the comfort of your own home and is an ideal solution if you have little time or money to spare. It gives you complete control over how long you spend, how much money you spend, and what you do. Your home mini-retreat could be ten minutes lying on a bed, listening to music, or reading a book. It could also involve activities like yoga, meditation, and home beauty treatments.

The primary aim of the retreat is to set an *intention*. What needs are you trying to meet with your retreat? What do you feel has been lacking in your life, and what are you yearning for? If you are aware of these things while you plan and prepare for your retreat, you are far more likely to meet your needs.

To get inspiration for your mini-retreat, look at an actual retreat you would take if time and money were no object. Then, it's time to get creative. How can you recreate this in a way that meets your current needs? You can make your mini-retreat as complex or as simple as you want, as long or as short as you desire. I have spent mini-retreats knitting, crafting, meditating, journaling, watching a few episodes of my current favorite TV show, painting my nails, and more.

A home mini-retreat is less about what you do or how long it lasts, and more about what you want to get from it. I often feel internal pressure to be "productive," so these times are a chance to give myself permission to relax. The important thing is to focus on the feelings and experience you want. Once you know what you want the *effect* of your home mini-retreat to be, you're in a much better position to plan how to create those feelings.

3: Write a letter to your future self

Writing a letter to your future self is a simple but effective exercise. You can do it when you feel you want to, or if you know you have a time coming up during which you're going to need an extra boost. You can write your letter by hand, send it in an email, or simply save it as a document on your computer. As you write your letter, think of your "best self." Why would you describe that version of yourself as your best self, and what do you appreciate about them?

To start, address yourself (e.g. "Dear Hannah,"), then continue from there. Be as positive and as charitable toward yourself as possible. Highlight the things about yourself that you like, appreciate, or are proud of. *Do not hold back or skip this part.* This letter is for you only, so don't worry about what other people would think if they read it: it's none of their business. It might feel uncomfortable, but sit with that discomfort and try to focus on what you like about yourself as a person, as opposed to what you've achieved. If it feels really uncomfortable, set a timer for five minutes. At the end of the five minutes, you can get up and walk away from your list. While that timer is running, however, you're going to sit, think about and write the things that make you "you," and why you appreciate and enjoy them.

Once you're finished, save your letter for when you need a dose of self-kindness and a reminder of everything you are.

4: The Have-Done list

I am a planner and, without my to-do list, I would be adrift. But I also acknowledge sometimes the more I do, the more I seem to have to do, which leads me to ask: 1) Where is it all coming from? and 2) How can I feel sane about this? Wait, let's dream big: how can I feel *good* about it? Other chapters in this book deal with number one, but this self-care suggestion is about number two. Enter the "Have-Done" list.

The "Have-Done" list offers a different perspective on productivity and accomplishment. Instead of focusing on everything that's left on the "To-Do" list, with the "Have-Done" list, we can make a list of *everything we've done* as well. I always feel much better about the day when I make a "Have-Done" list. It can contain any accomplishment of any size, from "Got out of bed," "Got to work on time," and "Successful sugar-free day," to "Completed that huge project I've been working on for months," "Asked my boss for a raise," and "Sent that hard-but-necessary email."

When I have a lot going on, it's easy to feel overwhelmed by all the things I have yet to do and how far I have yet to go, while overlooking how far I've already come. The "Have-Done" list is evidence we are making progress, no matter how slow it might feel. It reminds us to celebrate all that we are and all that we are doing, rather than focusing on all we're not and haven't yet done.

5. The "Good Things" jar

This is a simple practice you can start anytime. Take a jar (or other suitable receptacle). Every time you feel grateful for someone or something or when something good happens in your life, write it down on a slip of paper and put it in the jar.

Making time to acknowledge the things that are going well and the things we feel grateful for is a useful antidote when we're dwelling on all the things that are stressing us out. The things you include could range from huge things like telling someone you love them for the first time to small (but significant) things like the way the sunlight shone through the window when you got up this morning.

Once you have a few entries in your jar, revisiting these entries can itself become part of your self-care routine. Whenever you need a pick-me-up, simply open up your jar and start reading.

6. Enlist support

A common pattern among most people who struggle with self-kindness (including myself) is they believe they should be able to do everything alone. Asking for help and support can feel uncomfortable, as can receiving and accepting it without judging ourselves. When we're used to doing everything solo, it can feel vulnerable, even risky, to let other people support us, even for a while.

But, as musician and performance artist Amanda Palmer explains in both her popular TED talk and book, *The Art of Asking*, people often appreciate us giving them the opportunity to let them support us. Help is a gift. If others want to offer it, they will say so, and they won't be burdened or irritated if you say yes (and if they are, that's their responsibility). If they're not in a position to offer it, they'll say no. Either way, when we decide in advance other people are too busy or important to help us, we're making that decision for them without giving them a chance to consider it themselves. Let the people who care about you most choose.

7. The "WYCWYC" approach

When life is busy, it can feel like there's no way we can do all the things we want to do when we want to do them. A busy season at work, family commitments, health issues, or a multitude of other all-consuming things can all throw us into a tailspin. During these times, the things that are important but not urgent can slip down your list into the territory of, "Realistically, I'll never get around to this." Not doing these things, though, can leave us feeling depleted, exhausted, and functioning at a lower level than we otherwise would. We don't have time to do these important-but-not-urgent things, yet without them, we are less able to tackle the things that are taking up our time in the first place.

In this situation, I use the "What you can, when you can" (WYCWYC) approach. As the name suggests, this involves doing what you can, when you can, and it's a great way to keep habits, activities and practices ticking along in the background while we are focusing on other things. The beauty of the WYCWYC approach is that it's built on a series of tiny choices and doesn't take much effort in the moment. Over time, however, these choices snowball and compound into good habits and even better feelings.

In any moment, this might look like:

Choosing to take the stairs instead of the lift.

Choosing a salad instead of a burger.

Choosing to write instead of surf Facebook.

Choosing water over a soda.

Choosing to wait and think about it rather than buy today.

Choosing to walk instead of driving or taking public transport.

Choosing self-kindness over self-criticism.

None of these things are going to happen all the time. But the beauty of the WYCWYC approach is we take it one step at a time. Rather than setting unattainable standards or unrealistic rules for ourselves, we're focused on the choice in front of us. Tomorrow is tomorrow; what matters is right now.

You might read this and think, "That's great and all, but this is the problem. I want to make changes, but I can't seem to make them stick." If this sounds familiar, hi, you're not alone! The next chapter is all about how to be kind to ourselves when we're struggling to make the changes we want to make.

Your moment of kindness:

Use the suggestions in this chapter to create an action plan for the next time you have a lot on your plate

What ideas resonate most with you?

How can you approach busy times from a place of self-kindness?

EIGHTEEN
HOW TO BE KIND TO YOURSELF WHEN YOU'RE STRUGGLING TO MAKE THE CHANGES YOU WANT TO MAKE

"If information was the answer then we'd all be billionaires with perfect abs."

—Derek Sivers

Most of us have changes we would like to make in our lives, yet doing so can feel hard. So hard, there are books, workshops, programs, livelihoods, and whole industries dedicated to making changes. And we still struggle!

When we're struggling to make changes, and don't understand why, we can feel even more out of control and helpless. In this chapter, you'll discover some of the most common reasons behind the struggle and a few ways we can approach this struggle with self-kindness. I'm a big believer that understanding leads to clarity and action. We don't want to stop and set up camp in the "understanding" phase. Putting that understanding into action is important, too, and you'll discover how to do that in this chapter. But understanding is an important stepping stone toward action and making the changes we want to make.

1. You're avoiding discomfort

Making changes comes with discomfort. Change can feel risky and the outcome uncertain. Making the change might require us to face all kinds of experiences we'd rather avoid: judgment, rejection, failure, and so on. I've found it useful to think about change from a perspective described by writer Srinivas Rao: change isn't about how much you want it, it's about how uncomfortable you're willing to be to make it happen. The less willing we are to feel uncomfortable, the less sticky the change will be. I've found it helpful to ask myself: *how uncomfortable am I willing to be to make this change happen?* If the truthful answer is: "Not very..." then it's time to reconsider whether this is a change I want to make (as opposed to something I think I should be doing).

If you want to make a change but the perceived discomfort feels overwhelming, break the change down into smaller steps. Rather than committing to change your career, could you start by researching re-training opportunities? Rather than signing up for a 12-week fitness bootcamp, can you commit to going for a 20-minute walk each day first instead? Just like the procrastination I wrote about in "How to Be Kind to Yourself When You're Finding it Hard to Get Motivated," anticipating the experience of discomfort often feels worse than the discomfort itself. This isn't the case for every change—some changes come with a challenging transition period. But, for most everyday changes, living in anticipation of doing something uncomfortable is, ironically, often much more uncomfortable than doing the uncomfortable thing.

How can you break the change down into tiny steps? What would the first one be?

2. You're experiencing fear of the unknown

What will happen if you make this change? We often focus on the potential downside: what if I fail? What if this doesn't work out? But alongside this, we can also have fears based on a very different outcome too: *What if I succeed?* What if this changes other areas of my life? What if I make the change, then don't enjoy it? What if I make the change, then screw it up, lose everything, and end up back where I started? What if my partner/girlfriend/boyfriend/parents/siblings/co-workers/pets don't like this change?

As well as paying attention to your fears around negative outcomes, give voice to the fears around success, too. Every change—even the best, most life-enhancing changes—come with some loss and grieving for the path not taken. When I try to pretend these things don't exist or tell myself I should feel happy/grateful/excited (regardless of how I actually feel), I'm more likely to avoid the change. Giving these feelings and fears a voice before moving forward at least helps me feel I'm working with myself, rather than against myself.

Once you've given voice to these fears, go back and imagine your life one year, three years, five years from now. If you don't make this change, what will that life look like? How will you feel? And if you make this change, what will that life look like? How will you feel? Painting this picture can help you get clarity on whether the unknowns are worth facing to live the life you want to live.

What fears do you have around failure to make this change? What fears do you have around success if you were to make this change? How do you think it would affect other areas of your life?

3. You're trying to change too many things at once

As productivity coach David Allen says, "You can do anything, but not everything." I don't know about you, but when I have many changes I want to make in my life, I feel internal pressure to do all the things right now. I feel impatient to get from A to B and reap the rewards as quickly as possible. So I dive in headfirst, set myself an ambitious schedule of change, and wait for the magic to happen.

In reality, this isn't sustainable. Making one change, even a small one, can require all the mindfulness and effort we have to spare. Having self-awareness around the things we want to change and the ambition to do so is valuable, however, it's also important to remember: you have time. As valid as the YOLO/carpe diem mindset is, it can leave us feeling like we're behind compared to where we should be. Slow, steady, and sustainable progress that takes you toward where you want to be in the long-term is much better than a flurry of activity that burns out and leaves you feeling despondent and self-critical.

I've already talked about taking tiny steps a few times, and this applies here, too. If you're taking on too much change at once and feeling overwhelmed and stuck as a result, choose one change to focus on for the next month. At the end of that month, check in and see how it's going: do you need more time to focus on this change, or does it feel more manageable now? If you're dealing with a big change and a month feels too short a time, increase that time to three months. Give yourself space and slow down. You won't fall behind, you'll still be enough, you have time.

If you had to choose one thing to focus on now, what would that be?

4. You're seeking support and validation from the wrong people

Support is crucial for making changes. The bigger the change, the more support we need. When we're changing something meaningful about our lives, we want to make sure we have the right backing behind us.

By default, most of us turn to family and close friends. However, this isn't always the best source of support, especially if they are engaging in the patterns, activities, or dynamics you'd like to change, or their concern for you overrides their ability to be supportive. If your friends are all smokers and you decide you want to quit, they won't be the best people to support you (unless they're joining you). Equally, if your dream is to move to Fiji and set up a scuba-diving business, some family members might balk at the thought of you leaving a secure job and stable life for an uncertain future abroad. This doesn't mean you can't talk to them about your decision, but it's worth being mindful that they might have their own feelings, thoughts, beliefs, and fears that color their response. Instead, support might come from outside the circle of people we know, and a role model might not always be someone with whom we have a personal relationship. Instead, they might be someone who has trodden a similar path before us and is sharing their journey in public.

Finding the right support doesn't mean shunning anyone who disagrees with you. So-called naysayers have an important role. They can throw up helpful questions you might not have considered and force you to think through different aspects of the change. But there's helpful naysaying and unhelpful naysaying. We want to make sure we're disagreeing with people who will respect our individuality and help us grow.

Who do you know who can support you with this change? And who might make a good role model from a distance?

5. You are expecting change to be easy or instantaneous

Some changes are simple, but most are not, and it's often difficult to predict which changes will fall into either category. Making changes that seem like a piece of cake in theory might actually be teeth-grittingly difficult in practice. And that's OK. There is a difference between thinking, "This is going to be hard, and I don't know if I can go through with it," and "This is likely to be hard, and I believe I can do it."

Before my eldest child was born, my husband and I attended a birth preparation class. The most helpful piece of advice I took from it was: hope for the best and plan for the worst. It's good advice for birth—and life overall. You will slip up, things will get in the way, life happens, and it often takes grit and perseverance to continue whatever the weather. That's where planning for the worst can be useful.

As you approach your change, consider: what will you do when you slip up? What will your next step be? How will you respond when you're tempted to revert to your old pattern/behavior? How will you stick to the path you've chosen? Returning to the example of quitting smoking, you can ask, "How will I respond when I'm in a situation where other people are smoking? When I'm craving a cigarette, what will I do instead? What other activities can I engage in during those times until the craving passes?" Hope for the best, plan for the worst, and you'll find reality often lands somewhere in the middle.

If you were to hope for the best and plan for the worst, what would you do differently? How does this approach affect how you feel about making this change?

6. You are making changes from a place of "not good enough"

We already explored this in part one, when we discussed comparisonitis and perfectionism in "How to Be Kind to Yourself When You Feel 'Not Good Enough'," but I'll mention it again here because it's relevant. How you think about yourself matters, including the stories you attach to making (or not making) a particular change. When we decide it's time to change, we often do so through realizing something in our lives isn't working or we're no longer happy with the way things are. We might have reached rock bottom, or we might have arrived at a place of thinking to ourselves, "OK, that's enough now." If we're wanting to change something we don't feel good about, it's easy to slip into scarcity-based thinking and motivation. Perhaps we believe we're not good enough until we make a change, perhaps we believe other people would judge and reject us if they knew how hard this change was for us to make, or perhaps we are engaging in "when...then..." thinking (e.g. "*When* I lose 10 pounds, *then* I'll feel confident enough to date").

Setting goals and aspirations out of fear and scarcity is not conducive to happiness and life satisfaction. Here's something we forget with change and self-kindness: We can be self-accepting and still have things we want to do and ways in which we want to grow. We can believe we are enough and also want to explore our capabilities and potential further.

The changes we make from a place of believing we are already enough are a lot more fulfilling, life-enriching, and worthwhile.

*How would you approach this change if you were starting from a place of "good enough"? How would you feel if you shifted your perspective from "I'm doing this so I can feel worthy" to "I'm doing this **because** I am worthy."*

7. You're letting your inner critics rule the show

As I wrote about in *The Power of Self-Kindness: How to Transform Your Relationship With Your Inner Critic*, our inner critics mean well and are trying to protect us in their own ways. But they end up doing more harm than good. When we listen to the voices telling us we're useless, it's hopeless, why bother, etc., this won't help us change. It's more likely to cause us to slip into the "not enough" thinking I described above.

While there is no single solution to dealing with our inner critics, if yours are ruling the show, I invite you to challenge them. As I said right at the beginning of this book, I don't believe in telling our inner critics to shut up or calling them names (do you like it when someone does that to you? I don't), but it is important to set boundaries with them. If your inner critic is telling you how useless you are, encourage it to be a little more constructive. Ask questions like "So what would it look like to *not* be useless in this situation? What would you do instead?" Keep persevering with your questions and see what they offer in response.

What happens if you try to question your critics? Are there any other internal voices that come up that are more constructive too?

8. You're experiencing confirmation bias

We view new information, situations, and opportunities through the lens of what we already believe. In some situations, this can be helpful (for example, "assuming the best" is a lens I try to use). It can also be unhelpful. If we believe we aren't good enough, we will focus on experiences that (from our perspective) prove this belief, while filtering out experiences that contradict it. If, deep down, we don't think we can make the changes we want to make, we will look for information that confirms this and overlook anything that suggests otherwise.

The first step to overcoming confirmation bias is to notice it and to open ourselves up to *all* information. This includes that which confirms our existing beliefs and that which encourages us to create new ones. A tool I've found useful for doing this is practicing observing, rather than judging. This is something I'll talk about more in the chapter on How to Be Kind to Yourself in the Face of Rejection in the next section, but it's useful here, too. Observing is about stating the facts, while judging involves attaching meaning to those facts. It's the difference between "I'm still going to bed later than I planned," and "I'm still going to bed later than I planned… because I'm irresponsible, waste too much time in the evenings and can't even make a simple change like this." The next time you notice yourself spotlighting all the evidence that you can't make the change you want to make, ask yourself: "What's the evidence that I *can* do this?"

What existing beliefs are you bringing to this change? Are these helpful, or might they be getting in the way?

9. You have an external locus of control

Our "locus of control" describes the degree to which we feel we're in control over the events of our lives and our actions. An internal locus of control means we believe we have more control ourselves. With an external locus of control, we believe our lives are primarily influenced by external factors and fate. Where our locus falls on the spectrum isn't determined how much control we *say* we think we have, but how we actually behave.

We don't inhabit a fixed point on the internal-external scale: our sense of control and agency shifts from experience to experience. Most situations contain elements we can control and elements we can't; it helps us most when we pay attention to those we can. If someone rear-ends us at a set of traffic lights because they're busy texting, that's not something we can control. Making sure we have adequate insurance to cover the repair costs is.

When we have an external locus of control, we feel at the mercy of other people, our environment, and other external forces. This mindset makes it harder to make the changes we want to make because we feel like we're always being blown off course by things we can't do anything about. This can leave us feeling helpless, demotivated, and stuck. If we have an external locus of control, we're more likely to blame not making changes we want to make on being too busy, a lack of support from other people, the time of year, the economy, etc.

With an internal locus of control, we're more likely to explore what we can control and influence within the situation. If we're too busy, how can we free up more time to focus on our desired change? If our partner isn't giving us the support we want, can we try talking to them about it, or seek support elsewhere? If it's raining all week, can we go running indoors or invest in some wet-weather gear? If we're having trouble finding a new job, how can we change where we're looking or what we're looking for to improve our chances?

Where is your locus of control? If you think it might be external, what is one thing you can do differently today to shift toward an internal locus of control?

10. You're doing what worked for someone else, not what works for you

As I mentioned above, role models can be helpful. At the same time, it's worth remembering that what worked for them on their journey won't always yield the same results for you on yours. Knowing when to heed the advice and when to say "thank you," and go your own merry way is an important part of becoming who you are. Trying to fit ourselves into a mold that isn't right for us will leave us feeling anxious, out of place, and stuck.

I've found this hard. If someone sounds like they know what they're talking about, I think they must know better than me—especially with areas in which I already lack confidence. Not always the case! I often have to remind myself that I'm the one living my life, no one else, and I have permission to go my way, in my style, and in my timeframe.

So how do we tell the difference between advice and guidance that's helpful and that which isn't a good fit for us? Speaking from hard-won personal experience, I've found more often than not it's a question of "try it on and see." Beyond this, it usually comes down to three important criteria: values, credibility, and progress. Values means looking at what the person is doing or recommending through the lens of my values and what matters to me in my life. How do those things fit together? Do I want a life based on that other person's values and the choices they've made? Credibility is also important: do they walk their talk (and how long have they been walking it for?). If so, how is that working out for them? If not, why are they giving advice they haven't followed or don't follow themselves? Finally, progress involves asking: "Does this advice match where I am on my journey?"

Who have you been looking to for advice and guidance so far? What of their advice has worked, and which do you think you might be better leaving behind?

11. You have a fixed mindset

Growing up, I believed I was unathletic. This belief was rooted in a fixed mindset: I thought you either were athletic or you weren't, and I was in the "not" camp. That belief also came with a smidgen of shame. So I would avoid any situation that came with the potential to show my so-called innate lack of athleticism and stay in my comfort zone.

As an adult, I've done many things that contradict that belief, whether that's cycling from London to Brighton, hiking up volcanoes, or doing two 8-week cycles of Insanity back-to-back. In fact, I am athletic and I love a good physical challenge. But until I changed my thinking about this from "you either have it or you don't" to "this is something I can improve over time," I didn't give myself the chance to try these experiences. The truth is most things we believe to be "fixed" about ourselves aren't. Intelligence, mindset, optimism, skills—these are all things we can influence and change. Before we can do that, though, we need to accept they are changeable. As long as we are holding on to beliefs that we're "not someone who is X" (athletic/creative/good with money/can lose weight/insert your own desired change here), we won't make the changes we want to make.

If it feels too hard to shift a negative story about the change you want to make, there is one word I invite you to add: *yet*. I'm not athletic... *yet*. I'm not good at talking to people... *yet*. I'm not (insert negative belief here)... *yet*. It's a small dose of the growth mindset, but the more you practice it, the more you'll get used to this way of thinking.

How do you feel about the change you want to make when you add "yet"? What would you do differently if you viewed this change as a growth process rather than a race to the finish line?

12. You don't really want to change (yet)

Sometimes, we kinda, sorta want to change, but we don't *want to* want to. And, if that's where you are, that's a fine place to be.

The saying "if you're not changing, you just don't want it enough" is popular in the personal growth and coaching worlds. It might look good as a pithy Instagram quote, but the reality is often far more nuanced and complicated. As I hope this chapter has shown, there are *many* reasons we encounter stumbling blocks when changing our lives. That's not even including physical and mental differences that might make certain changes harder or not possible. Suggesting that anytime we find change hard it's because we don't want it enough lacks understanding at best. At worst, it carries an undertone of shaming, even discrimination.

But, while this belief is problematic when applied universally, there are certain situations in which it's true. Sometimes we think we want to make a change because that's what other people have told us we should do. Or, we're listening to old internal scripts about the way we should live and the person we should be. But we—our true selves—don't actually want to make that change. In that situation, not wanting to change isn't a sign you're lazy/a coward/a loser, but a sign you're listening to yourself and challenging those "shoulds."

We also might not have reached a point where the pain of staying where we are is greater than the pain of making the change. Who wants to trade less pain for more pain?! That doesn't mean we can't make the change, but if we're struggling and this is the reason, it's important to acknowledge and accept this is where we are right now.

If you're struggling to decipher where your desire to change is coming from, I invite you to return to the line of questioning I mentioned earlier in this chapter: If, one year from now, I haven't made this change, how am I going to feel? What is my life going to look like? What impact will it have on other areas of my life? What about five years from now? What about 10 years?

And, if I do make this change, how am I going to feel one year from now? What is my life going to look like? What impact will it have on other areas of my life? What about five years from now? What about 10 years? As well as thinking about your responses to these questions, allow yourself to feel your emotional response, too. Put yourself in the shoes of Future You one, five and 10 years from now. Imagine what it would feel like to be them; which is closer to how you want to feel?

Take a moment to answer the questions above: If you haven't made this change one year from now, what will your life look like? What about five years? 10 years? And, if you have made this change one year from now, what will your life look like? What about five years? 10 years?

13. You're looking for the "one thing"

Change usually takes time. This isn't a popular reality, hence the proliferation of books, courses and gurus who try to sell you on the idea there is *one thing* that will transform your life and make all your troubles disappear. This mindset is so enticing that I know it's not true, yet I still have to remember to view these kinds of messages through my critical thinking glasses. If you're someone for whom change doesn't come easy (most of us), it can leave you wondering whether there's something wrong with you. In reality, that one thing doesn't exist.

The good news is wherever you're starting from, change *can* happen. There won't be a cure-all that will solve your problems and change your life for the better. It's likely to be a combination of things, plus dedicated effort on your part. But it is possible and yours for the taking. Whatever change you're wanting to make, and whatever obstacles you've come up against so far, know this: the possibility of change comes with each new breath. It starts now, whether it's 8 am or 10 pm, Monday or Thursday, December or July.

To borrow a saying from a friend, "Every moment is the chance to do something differently." What are you going to do differently today?

How does this change how you perceive the change you're trying to make? What is one thing you want to do differently today?

Your moment of kindness:

Think of a change you're struggling with in your life right now: which of the reasons above resonate most with you?

Based on this awareness, how would you like to approach this change differently from now on?

NINETEEN
HOW TO BE KIND TO YOURSELF WHEN YOU DON'T DO WHAT YOU SAY YOU'RE GOING TO DO

Never forget that once upon a time, in an unguarded moment, you recognized yourself as a friend.

—Elizabeth Gilbert, *Eat Pray Love: One Woman's Search for Everything*

We've all had the experience of making a commitment or agreement, then either not fulfilling it or doing the bare minimum because our heart isn't in it. I know I find it hard to say "no" because I don't want to disappoint someone or miss out on an opportunity, only to realize I don't have time or it's taking energy away from other things that are more important. But the fallout from not being committed, even if it's internal fallout for me, is usually far more uncomfortable than it would have been to say "no."

Doing what we say we're going to do when we say we're going to do it is one of the most basic forms of integrity. When we don't fulfill this commitment, it can affect our relationships and damage our trust in ourselves, too. But we are human, we drop balls, life happens and we make decisions we later regret. Facing up to unfulfilled commitments can be a painful process but, in the long term, it's the kindest and most helpful thing we can do. Here are five ways you can be kind to yourself when you don't do what you say you're going to do:

1. Acknowledge why

If we say we will do something, then don't, there's a reason. Part of responding with self-kindness is to be curious with ourselves about what that reason could be. Questions to ask and answer as honestly as possible include:

1. How did you feel when thinking about this commitment or agreement?
2. What else was happening in your life?
3. What really stopped you from meeting this commitment? (Hint: was it you? A decision you made? Leaving something too late? A story you told yourself? Sometimes, it is external circumstances, but this is also an opportunity to look at the elements you had control over.)
4. If this wasn't something you wanted, or had the time, to do, why do you think you made the agreement or commitment?

If you can't identify any obvious external factors, think about the feelings underneath your resistance or avoidance. Did you notice feeling some fear or worry around the commitment? Did you feel out of your depth? Did you feel overwhelmed? Approach this exploration from a place of self-compassion. We all have our blind spots, and the more we can direct attention and compassion to them, the more likely we are to be aware of them in the future.

2. Decide how you'd like to make amends

As I mentioned in "How to Be Kind to Yourself When You Make a Mistake," making amends is more than apologizing (although that's important, too!), it's about taking action to repair the situation. What action can you take to make amends in this situation? Sometimes this might look like honoring the original commitment, but learning from the situation so you can choose better next time. Sometimes it looks like acknowledging you can't do what you said you'd do, but suggesting someone else who can, or offering to meet the other party halfway with a compromise. What you do will depend on the situation, but it's always better to approach the other people involved with a solution, not just a problem.

3. Adjust your boundaries

Piling too much onto our plates then getting angry and/or frustrated with ourselves when we can't finish the whole meal isn't fair. If you repeat this pattern, try to unpack the underlying beliefs that contribute to this cycle. What is the worst-case scenario if you say no to something? What would happen if you stopped feeling stressed/over-worked/over-committed? What would be different in your life if you were someone who finished things and honored commitments? How would that feel? This also applies to how we feel about other people. Agreeing to do things then feeling resentful and angry with the person/people who asked you to do them is a sign you are due for a boundary adjustment. We are the gatekeepers of our time. Whether you make an agreement or commitment is your responsibility, no matter how persuasive other people are. Although these feelings can be uncomfortable, they contain a message. Feelings are like our internal GPS, telling us it's time for a change in direction, whether that's related to how we're thinking about a situation, or extra boundaries we need to put in place.

4. Prepare for what you'll do differently next time

Whatever has happened in the past, we can always do things differently in the future. If something stopped you from doing what you said you were going to do this time, what can you change next time to make sure it doesn't happen again? Decide now, make your steps clear and actionable, and commit to starting them today.

Your moment of kindness:

Think back to a time when you didn't do what you said you were going to do? What happened?

How did you feel about it?

How could you have been kinder to yourself in that situation?

What can you learn from that experience for the next time this happens?

TWENTY
HOW TO BE KIND TO YOURSELF WHEN IT'S HARD TO DETACH SELF-WORTH FROM PRODUCTIVITY

Measure your worth by your dedication to your path, not by your successes and failures.

—Elizabeth Gilbert, *Big Magic*

It's the weekend. I have some sacred alone time. I am exhausted and want to curl up with my latest Netflix series and knitting project. But my downtime plans are not appreciated by one of my internal voices: *You should use this time to work on your book! This would be a great opportunity to clear out that cupboard that's been bugging you for weeks! Look at all these things you wanted to get done this week and haven't yet! Are you going to fritter this precious time away on relaxing!?*

Sometimes the answer is clear: You bet I am. But sometimes the nagging gets to me and, guilt-ridden, I begrudgingly get up to do whatever this voice is telling me I should do, feeling resentful and unenthusiastic about doing it.

Detaching self-worth from productivity is hard... except, I realized when I started exploring the ideas I talk about in this chapter, it's not. Detaching self-worth from busy-ness is hard. But, when we separate out "busy" and "productive," two things that are often conflated but in reality very different, the issue becomes clearer.

When we assume that productivity means "spending time on things that matter to us," it's clear that our level of productivity can influence our sense of self-worth. But we want to detach from busy-ness for the sake of being busy. An activity or pursuit is only productive if it's actually adding something to our lives. Busy work (work that keeps us occupied but doesn't move us closer to our goal) is attractive. It's something our culture prides and expects, but it's not in our best interests to buy into the narrative that busy equals better or more worthy.

With that in mind, here are a few ways we can detach our sense of self-worth from how busy we are.

1. Reframe rest

The problem with my internal voice in the situation above is she believes rest is frivolous, verging on self-indulgent. But she's wrong. If you want to grow flowers, you need to plant seeds first. Once they're in the soil, there is a period where not much seems to be happening on the surface. But underneath, a new life is beginning, energy is being released, and big changes are taking place. We are the same. To live full lives, we need those times to plant and nurture the seeds of whatever is coming up next for us. This is what rest is all about and, in this light, it is a priority.

2. Adopt self-worth as a value, not a condition

What we do and who we are (and whether those things match up to our values and our sense of who we should be) influence our sense of self-worth. But, somewhat counterintuitively, deepening our sense of self-worth becomes easier when we hold self-worth as a value, not as the result of something conditional. When we view self-worth as a condition, we do X, Y, and Z to feel worthy. When we start by holding our sense of self-worth as one of our most important values, we are starting from a place of being enough. We already acknowledge the importance of self-worth. We do the things we want to do *because* we honor and value our self-worth, not because we're trying to earn it.

The things we do because we value our self-worth might be similar, but the energy behind them is quite different. It's avoiding pain (in this case, the pain of not feeling worthy) versus seeking growth (starting from a place of having self-worth as a key value).

3. Filter out the activities that don't add value to your life

I don't know about you, but I have go-to distractions when I'm feeling tired, drained, or anxious about something (distractions that usually involve my phone). These things don't help me feel less tired, drained, or anxious. They add little to my life, and I usually feel worse after doing them than I did before. Instead of letting these activities take control, I'm trying to be more mindful of what I default to. Then, I can replace activities that bring me no joy and don't meet my needs with those that do (reading a book, working on a craft project, drinking a glass of water, etc.).

4. Eat the frog

I feel the most icky about the self-worth/busy relationship when I know I'm procrastinating on something important. I do a lot of the busy work I mentioned earlier while procrastinating. This helps me feel like I'm making progress but doesn't actually get me closer to my goals.

"Eat the frog" is a phrase coined by productivity author Brian Tracy, who uses it to describe doing the most important things on your task list first. There are lots of tried and tested techniques for overcoming procrastination. My favorite is setting the bar low and telling myself I can stop after 10 minutes. 10 minutes isn't much, but even if I take one step toward a big project or task I've been putting off, that's still one step I hadn't taken before.

10 minutes is also enough to remind myself of the big truth behind procrastination, one that I already mentioned in the previous chapter. The discomfort that comes from avoiding something is usually greater than the discomfort associated with doing that thing.

5. Follow what is right for you, not what you think you *should* do

These days, we can see so much of other people's lives, activities, and pursuits through social media and online. This can be a gift. We get to see what people are doing and how they are doing it. It's an opportunity to see behind-the-scenes processes that were previously only available to a select few. But this transparency also has a downside. We're bombarded by other people's goals, definitions of success, and what the "right" way to live looks like to *them*.

When I started working for myself many moons ago, I looked to other people to tell me what to do, and didn't always look in the right places. Now I'm a decade into this journey, I'm better able to filter out the noise and have less insecurity around needing other people's validation or advice. I still value role models, feedback, learning, and growth—but from the right sources. During this time, I've also become a mother. Now, I have less time to work, but I'm far more productive in the time I have. Our goals and definitions also change. In 10 years' time, I might have different goals. My definition of success might have changed, and I might work toward these things in a different way, too. But just because a certain approach or path is "normal" or what everyone else is doing doesn't mean it's right for you. Remember the condition of comparisonitis: we can't necessarily stop comparing ourselves to others, but we don't want to try to catch up or compete with the people we compare ourselves to either. Instead, we can use our comparison to signpost us to changes we might want to make based on our own values and goals.

6. Focus on the process

Like the quote from Elizabeth Gilbert at the beginning of this chapter says, our sense of self-worth comes from showing up for the things that are important to us.

That is enough.

I've mentioned the concept of falling in love with the process in previous chapters. I want to return to it here because it applies to detaching self-worth from productivity too.

In most situations, we can't control the outcome. The only thing we can control is how much time and effort we apply to the process. We set ourselves up for heartache when we base our sense of self-worth on something we can't control, and this includes the outcome of most situations. Instead, find value in the process, in the showing up, and in your dedication to yourself and what matters to you.

This chapter marks the end of part two, which has been all about doing. We've looked at how to be kind to ourselves in the face of external challenges and situations we might encounter as we go about our daily life. Over the last few chapters, we've learned how to be kind to ourselves when setting goals, making mistakes, and making changes. We've also looked at the topics of confidence, self-care, productivity, and motivation. The next section's theme is being. We'll be looking at situations and experiences in which existing as a person in the world can feel hard and exploring ways to be kind to ourselves in the process. Before that, though, here is your moment of kindness for this chapter.

Your moment of kindness:

Which of the suggestions above resonate most with you? Choose two you will try.

PART 3
BEING

TWENTY-ONE
HOW TO BE KIND TO YOURSELF WHEN YOU FEEL YOU'RE LACKING PURPOSE

> Your calling will never demand that it be the way you pay your mortgage. It is simply begging for some amount of expression in your life.
>
> —Tara Mohr

You've probably heard the rallying cry to "Follow your passion!" While this cry comes from a well-meaning place, plenty of people hear this call and think: *But what if I don't know what my passion is? What if I want a deeper sense of purpose in my life, but I don't know where to start?*

Some people have no problem identifying their vocation, their raison d'être, their calling in life. For some of us, though, identifying *the thing* that is our purpose can feel like a lot of pressure.

First, purpose is a big word. While we might have several things we're interested in pursuing further, none of them might feel like our "purpose." We might also know that the thing we're passionate about today, this month, this year, will change. We are constantly evolving and so do our interests and priorities. Perhaps it doesn't feel right to pick your *one thing* right now and close the door on everything else.

If you feel pressured to find your purpose, are uncertain of what your purpose might be, or are avoiding the topic altogether, this chapter is for you. What you're experiencing is less to do with you and more to do with what you've internalized—through no fault of your own—about the whole concept of purpose. For a gentler, kinder approach to cultivating a sense of purpose and meaning in your life, keep reading.

Purpose isn't something you find, it's something you create

The concept of "finding" your purpose is a misnomer. It's unlikely you'll be walking down the street one day, stumble over something, and look down to realize: Hey! It's your sense of purpose. Instead, a kinder way of thinking about where purpose fits in your life is that it's something you *create*. As we'll talk about more later in this chapter, this involves getting out into the world and trying lots of new things. It involves experimentation, openness, and permission to be wrong. Some people can work through a set of coaching exercises and come out the other side with clarity about what adds a sense of purpose to their life. But most of the time, this clarity comes from trying new things and seeing what sticks.

If you've been waiting for a sense of purpose, it's time to stop. It won't find you; nor can you force yourself to find it.

Plant the seeds of meaning. Start paying attention to yourself and the things that spark your interest. Notice when you're curious about something, whether that's advanced pottery-making techniques, horticulture, relationships, or forensic science. Look for patterns that come up in your life. Do you always gravitate to certain kinds of places, stories, people, subjects? What draws you to them?

As psychologist and author Eric Maisel wrote in an article published on *The Good Men Project*, "Treat your life as a project, as an opportunity to make yourself proud, and as an adventure foisted upon you by nature."

Purpose usually dwells in the small things

As children, most of us can remember having big dreams (mine were to be a popstar and a vet, at the same time). In reality, though, most of us are not high-flying, super-achieving recipients of fame and fortune. And nor would we want to be. While the relative financial security might be nice, the realities of living that kind of life would likely not leave us feeling fulfilled and content. Instead, we live quietly extraordinary lives. Quiet because often the most meaningful moments usually are those that very few other people see or know about. Extraordinary because no one else lives life quite like us.

Much of the talk around purpose in our culture today involves grand statements like "Find your passion, change the world!" But most of the time, our most meaningful moments won't involve radical achievements or life-altering experiences. And just because they don't involve these things, that doesn't make them less valid as a source of purpose. Big goals and dreams have their place. When we focus on making them happen at the expense of paying attention to the smaller things, though, we miss out. We have opportunities to create meaning and a sense of purpose every day, whether or not we achieve our biggest goals.

What gives you a sense of purpose will change and evolve

You can't find a sense of purpose and you can't lose it, either. What can happen—and probably will—is your sense of purpose will change. *You* will change. Over time, we amass a wealth of new experiences, perspectives, knowledge, meeting new people, and learning more about the world. With all this, it's natural that we grow and develop as people, and it's natural that our sense of purpose grows and evolves, too.

The idea there is one thing that is *your thing* isn't helpful to most of us. In fact, it can feel downright scary, because what if we never find that one thing? Or what if the thing we thought was our thing turns out not to be? What then? I worked with coaching clients who thought they might know what their *thing* was, but didn't want to explore that thing further. They didn't want to discover it wasn't actually their *thing* and find themselves back at square one, now with not even an idea or possibility to hold on to.

When we can embrace the idea that our sense of purpose will develop and change over time, we can stop clinging to the myth of the "one thing." We can give ourselves permission to let go of the things we've outgrown, the things that no longer fit into our lives, and the things that we no longer enjoy. We can acknowledge we're not the same person we were when we took up that activity or embarked on that project.

Your sense of purpose will be multi-faceted

There are many things that add a sense of purpose to my life. These include big things like my kids, writing, and learning something new. They also include smaller pursuits, like starting a new knitting project or re-organizing a space in my home. All these different things take up more or less space on the purpose spectrum, but they all contribute something. If I go too long without making something, I feel twitchy. I can't imagine not spending time with my kids. I would feel like I was missing something if I stopped writing. Learning and growth are also important to me.

This is another way in which the advice to "find your one thing" is problematic: most of us have many things. We are complex, multi-faceted beings, and so there will be a multitude of things that add a sense of purpose to your life in ways both big and small. Remove any of them, and you feel you lose something. If you've been feeling like your life is lacking a sense of purpose, is that because you have been expecting yourself to find the one thing that is your thing? If so, take a step back and start noticing the tiny threads of meaning that already run through your day-to-day activities.

Your purpose doesn't have to be how you earn money

We live in an age where gatekeepers are disappearing and we have more opportunities than ever to make a living doing what we love. With those opportunities, however, comes the pressure to monetize everything we enjoy and are good at. Sometimes this pressure is the helpful nudge we need toward taking a leap into the unknown and creating a meaningful career. After all, if we're good at something and we enjoy doing it, why wouldn't we want to earn money from it? If we are living our purpose, shouldn't that be the way we earn money, too?

Well, no, not always. As anyone who has "turned pro" with something they enjoyed knows, transitioning into the professional realm can change your relationship with that activity. Sometimes, it works, but sometimes, it doesn't. An activity that's fun as a hobby can become a stressful, soul-sucking drain on your life when it's something you rely on to earn a living.

I am the first person to celebrate the opportunities we now have, and I'm grateful to be living and working during the age of the Internet. But just because you could earn a living doing what you love doesn't mean you have to. As the quote at the beginning of this chapter illustrates, the things that give us a sense of purpose don't also need to be the things that pay our bills. They just need some kind of presence in our lives.

Creating a sense of purpose (without a sense of pressure)

Having explored some myths around purpose and the reality behind them, I want to offer some practical suggestions you can use to create a sense of purpose without the pressure:

Follow your curiosity

This advice comes from Elizabeth Gilbert, who wrote about this approach as an alternative to the traditional "follow your passion" mantra in her book *Big Magic*. As she explains, "In seasons of confusion, of loss, of boredom, of insecurity, of distraction, the idea of 'passion' can feel completely inaccessible... But curiosity, I have found, is always within reach."

Look for the things that speak to you in the everyday. Pursue your interests. Forget conventional wisdom and go where your attention draws you. There is no "right" way to do your most important work, so follow your own path and see where it leads...

Create a "new things" list

Each year, around the time of her birthday, writer and teacher Sarah Von Bargen creates a "new things" list for the 12 months ahead. At the time of writing, the items on her list range from making mayonnaise from scratch to taking a dance class with her husband and doing a candle-lit cross-country ski trail. This is following your curiosity in action. Not everything on her list is likely to be life-changing (or even turn out to be fun). But she is challenging herself to try new things and see what happens.

Go on Artist Dates

Artist Dates are a weekly commitment to take yourself out and do something that interests and intrigues you. They are a window for inspiration, rejuvenation, and remembering how to play—something most of us forget to do as adults.

An artist date might involve taking a trip to a local art gallery to peruse at your leisure for a couple of hours. It might involve setting aside an afternoon to cut interesting words, phrases and images out of magazines and create a collage for the fun of it. Artist dates do not have to involve "serious" creative endeavors (in fact, it's better if they don't).

As Julia Cameron, creator of *The Artist's Way* (and the concept of artist dates) explains: "The Artist Date need not be overtly 'artistic'—think mischief more than mastery... Ask yourself, 'what sounds fun?'—and then allow yourself to try it."

If you'd like a year's worth of ideas for Artist Dates to inspire your own practice, you can find a link to this in the Resources list at the end of this book and at http://www.becomingwhoyouare.net/htbk-resources.

Spend time with yourself

In our hyper-connected world, most of us spend more time turned outward in receiving mode rather than turned inward, in reflective mode. Make time to be with yourself and reconnect with everything that makes you *you*. Take a screen-free day (including your phone). Go out for a walk without your headphones in. Try journaling, meditation, or another reflective activity that encourages you to turn inward. When you turn off the noise, what comes through in the quiet?

If you've been struggling to separate your sense of purpose from what other people value, you'll find the next chapter on people-pleasing relevant, too. Very few of the topics and challenges I've included in this book exist in isolation. Most are interconnected and interwoven throughout the different facets of our lives. As you keep reading, I invite you to think about what approaching these challenges with more self-kindness might look like for you.

Your moment of kindness:

Which of these suggestions can you use to create a deeper sense of purpose in your life?

What would following your curiosity look like to you?

TWENTY-TWO
HOW TO BE KIND TO YOURSELF WHEN THE URGE TO PEOPLE-PLEASE IS STRONG

When you say *yes*, make sure you're not saying *no* to yourself.

—Paulo Coelho

You've probably heard the advice that we should stop caring so much about what other people think. Like the advice to follow our passion in the previous chapter, this comes from a well-meaning place. But it's neither a healthy approach nor realistic. Even if we could switch off this social drive like a light switch (which we can't), empathy is a wonderful and necessary social skill. If we were to take this advice at face value and stop caring what other people thought, we'd damage our closest relationships. We'd also be fulfilling one criterion used by forensic psychologists to determine levels of psychopathy (which I don't think is something any of us are aiming for).

Contrary to common advice, desiring approval from others isn't the psychological disaster it's made out to be. We can stumble into murky territory with validation, but the problem isn't caring what people think. What causes trouble—in our relationship with ourselves and other people—is depending on other people's validation as a substitute for our own and depending on the wrong people for validation. This usually results in what we would describe as "people-pleasing" behavior and is a sign of a deeper issue in our relationship with ourselves. In this chapter, I want to explore people-pleasing, the desire for validation, and how we can move through both these things toward genuine connection.

The major issue with people-pleasing

Let's start with a counterintuitive but important fact: people-pleasing doesn't work—even when we get what we want. When we change or hide things about ourselves to get validation from other people, we don't feel any better, even if we get their validation. We know, deep down, that the person they are validating is not us, it's who we're pretending to be.

This kind of validation seeking has a darker side too: it's controlling behavior. We are trying to control what other people think of us and, to a lesser but still important degree, how they behave toward us. We people-please because we don't want to experience rejection and feel all the uncomfortable feelings that arise from that. But what other people think, feel, and do isn't something we can control. Trying to do so not only sends the message to ourselves that we're not good enough as we are, but isn't respectful or fair to the other person either. The only thing we can control is how we show up and how we behave.

Are you giving yourself the validation you seek from others?

We are social beings, and it's natural to care about what people think. But we don't want to apply this indiscriminately, because not everyone knows us, understands us, or shares our values. I care about what my husband thinks because his feelings and thoughts matter to me. Taking them into account is part of maintaining a good relationship. Ditto for my friends. I also care about what my kids think because their wellbeing and growth are my responsibility.

But my hairdresser? She gives good haircuts, but I'm not about to change my life plans based on her opinions. We want to care about what the *right* people think. These are the people who have credibility, who we know are invested in our growth, and with whom we've built a well of trust.

When we seek validation from anyone and everyone, it's because there's a part of us that doesn't accept ourselves. When our internal world lacks acceptance and understanding, it's natural we turn to our external world to get it. Our job is to identify what that part is, what it's struggling with, and negotiate with ourselves toward self-acceptance first. We can do this by noticing:

When do I seek approval from other people?

What am I seeking approval for? (My career, appearance, specific life choices)

How do I want other people to see me?

Where do I feel I need to alter or hide parts of myself in to win acceptance and approval?

What does this tell me about what I'm not accepting about myself?

What are the beliefs I have about why I don't accept these aspects of myself?

What do I know to be true about these aspects of myself? How would I like to feel about them?

What would I like to believe about them?

If we're validating ourselves, we don't need validation from everyone around us. Will there be times when we need reassurance? Yes. Support? Absolutely. But we won't depend on other people's opinions to feel good about ourselves. When we are mindful of giving ourselves the approval we are seeking from others, we have greater freedom to be who we are.

Am I seeking connection or validation?

While we're in hot pursuit of validation, we miss out on something that is a core human need: connection.

It's a desire for connection (wanting to see and be seen) that drives our desire for relationships, but a desire for validation (wanting to be liked) that influences how we show up in those relationships. Belonging and acceptance are two of our core human needs. While these needs encourage us to behave well, and in this way support our relationships, we also want to keep them in perspective. As we've already examined, if we don't meet these needs through connection, we'll try to meet them through seeking validation (usually when we're not showing acceptance and belonging toward ourselves).

When we're willing to take a risk, detach ourselves from the need for approval, and show up as ourselves, we give ourselves the opportunity to connect with people on a meaningful level. We won't receive validation every time, but when we do, it's going to be deeper, more fulfilling, and real. Whenever I'm in an interaction with someone and I notice that anxious energy that comes with feeling like I need someone to like me, I ask myself: Am I seeking connection or validation here? Often, taking a moment to pause and ask this of myself helps me reset. Then, I can get back to the thing that not only strengthens my relationships but meets my needs: connection.

The next chapter is also about connection—connection with ourselves. We'll be discussing walking a psychological tightrope as we balance self-acceptance with the things we want to change.

Your moment of kindness:

Where do you need to give yourself approval first? Where might you be looking to other people to validate you instead?

Do you seek connection or validation? If it's the latter, what could you do differently next time the opportunity for connection arises?

TWENTY-THREE
HOW TO BE KIND TO YOURSELF WHEN YOU'RE STRUGGLING TO BALANCE SELF-ACCEPTANCE & SELF-IMPROVEMENT

> The first step toward change is awareness. The second step is acceptance.
>
> —Nathaniel Branden

Personal growth is full of paradoxes. One of the biggest is the tension between self-acceptance vs. self-improvement. I experience this tension regularly: I want to be the best version of myself and I also want to be OK with the way I am right now. I want a better, brighter future full of dreams, aspirations, and goals, and I also want to feel happy with what I have in the present.

So how do we make peace with these two things? How do we balance the desire for self-acceptance vs. self-improvement?

You can have too much of a good thing

I notice I struggle with the questions above when I take either element to its extreme. If I focus too much on self-improvement, I fall into the "When… then…" thinking I mentioned in "How to Be Kind to Yourself When You Don't Feel Confident." *When* I make the next big change, *then* I'll be happy. *When* I meet a certain goal, *then* I'll have time to do more of the things I want to do.

If you're familiar with this pattern of thinking, no doubt you can insert several of your own examples here. The problem with this "When… then…" framework is that it's rooted in the belief we are not enough as we are. As Nathaniel Branden writes in his book *The Six Pillars of Self-Esteem*, "If my aim is to prove I am 'enough,' the project goes on to infinity because the battle was already lost on the day I conceded the issue was debatable."

Another way self-improvement can hurt rather than help us is when it's born out of comparison. Wanting to improve myself to compete with other people also comes from feeling "not enough" and is at odds with self-acceptance. When we base our sense of self-worth on where we lie in relation to others, we will always be able to find examples of where we fall short. The only measure of worth that matters comes from our internal barometer. *Did I live in alignment with my values and principles today? Did I show up as the person I want to be?*

If I focus only on self-acceptance, though, I deny a very important—and natural—part of myself that longs for growth. Several psychologists discuss the drive for self-actualization, including Abraham Maslow and Carl Rogers. It's a natural, healthy desire to have. There are things I want to change about my life, about my behaviors, reactions, and thought patterns, and that's OK. As humans, we're always evolving, both as a species and as individuals.

Rather than turning this desire for growth into a problem, let's explore how to integrate these two elements and use them to our benefit. Although they might seem like they conflict, together they create a beautiful foundation for healthy ambition and growth.

Self-acceptance vs. self-improvement is a false dichotomy

In fact, self-acceptance and the desire for growth are symbiotic: one needs the other. We need to accept where we are right now to grow.

Self-acceptance doesn't mean liking where we are or viewing our current situation with rose-tinted glasses. Rather, it involves acknowledging the reality of what is; the good and the bad. This includes acknowledging there might be certain things about ourselves we would like to change or improve. It also involves exploring the things we struggle to accept and approaching them with curiosity and an open mind. It also, crucially, involves accepting our desire to grow. Let's say I don't have the energy I normally have and I'm not feeling good. I know I haven't been eating as healthily as I would like or getting enough sleep and exercise. Is it kinder to say "This is the way I am, so I should accept it?" or to acknowledge that I'm not enjoying the changes I'm experiencing, and make improvements where I can to get back to a place where I'm feeling how I want to feel? True self-acceptance means accepting our current situation. It also means accepting our feelings about that situation, including a desire to change it.

How to balance self-acceptance vs. self-improvement

Both self-acceptance and self-improvement come from one source: self-regard. This means wanting the best for ourselves—not because of what someone else is doing and not because we need to make up for something we feel we're lacking, but wanting the best because we have a place in this world, one life to live, and we're right in the middle of living it.

Notice your intention for wanting to make improvements.

Do they come from a place of wanting to optimize your life, or from wanting to fill some perceived internal lack? If it's the former, great. If it's the latter, you will find it more helpful to do some inner work around your sense of self-worth first. This might be something you do solo through reading books, journaling, and introspection. It might also be something you do with the support of a counselor or therapist. Shelve the self-improvement project as a secondary aim to focus on later. Ask yourself: *If I wanted the best for myself, what would I be doing differently right now?*

Start from your strengths.

I find it all too easy to focus on my weaknesses at the expense of keeping my strengths in mind, too. Self-acceptance involves looking at the whole package. It includes acknowledging our weaknesses but also being able to identify and focus on our strengths, too. Ask yourself: *What is going well right now? What am I happy with? What strengths do I already have that I can use to improve the things I want to improve?*

Think of the growth curve as a series of upticks and plateaus.

I've noticed after a period of intense personal growth, I need a period of rejuvenation. One way to think of this is that you are planting seeds now, ready for flowers to bloom in the future. Growth is like the seasons. Spring and summer are times of fertile growth. Fall and winter are necessary fallow time for recuperation and rejuvenation before the next growth cycle begins. The times you are not actively "growing" are as important as the times when you are. Ask yourself: *How can I become more conscious of my growth spurts and plateaus?*

Focus on the journey, not the destination.

There is no destination (unless you count death). Until then, everything is the journey. Life is not what happens in the future when we've lost 10 pounds or won that promotion or found the love of our lives. Life is happening right now. This very second! Focus on falling in love with the process, rather than the outcome. Ask yourself: *What needs to happen for me to appreciate and find value in the journey, this part I am living right now?*

If you don't like something, do something about it (from a place of self-kindness).

There comes a point when we've done enough reading and talking about what we want to change, and the only thing left to do is take action. Staying in the reading/talking phase only leads to frustration (and usually those "not enough" feelings—see how this is all interlinked?) Doing this from a place of self-kindness means making the changes as easy as possible, being honest with yourself about what's working and what's not. For me, this kind of transparency and accountability is an important part of self-kindness—when it's done from a positive and loving place. It's not easy to practice, but it's a necessary part of becoming who I am.

Your moment of self-kindness:

Think of an area of self-improvement that is currently weighing on your mind. How can you approach this with self-acceptance while also honoring your desire to grow?

TWENTY-FOUR
HOW TO BE KIND TO YOURSELF IN THE MIDDLE OF BIG TRANSITIONS

When you come out of the storm, you won't be the same person who walked in. That's what the storm's all about.

—Haruki Murakami

Transitions are a natural part of life and an inevitable part of being human. We encounter many big transitions throughout the course of our lives. Leaving home, changing jobs, breakups, getting married, moving house, having kids, and more can all shake our sense of stability. Some of these transitions we choose, some we don't. Some transitions run smoothly, others jolt us into an awareness of how fragile and tenuous life can feel, and how little control we have over it. Transitions can be a source of possibility and opportunity, or like being KO'ed by a monster wave. Whatever the transition looks like, even positive transitions can cause emotional upheaval. If we can be kind to ourselves when everything feels like it is in flux, though, we can emerge stronger and more resilient. That's what this chapter is all about.

Focus on what's going well, rather than on what's not

As humans, we are natural problem-solvers. Focusing on the negative is a survival mechanism and therefore automatically kicks in during times of stress and/or change (and, let's be real, outside of times of stress and change too; that negative bias is everywhere!). When we focus on the negative, however, we risk succumbing to what psychologist Shawn Achor describes in his book, *The Happiness Advantage*, as "The Tetris Effect."

The name for this effect comes from the phenomenon that occurs when people play a lot of Tetris. They see opportunities for everyday, real-life objects to fit together similarly to blocks in the game. Emotionally, this means when we focus on stress, negativity, and failure, we see it everywhere. We become blind to the positive, exacerbating our stressful and negative experience of life.

I try to counteract my tendency to catastrophize by taking time to focus on what's going well, too. This helps my mind to focus on the possibilities and potential that come with a particular transition. It isn't about ignoring problems—problem-solving is a necessary and useful skill. Instead, it's about ensuring we're also open to positive outcomes and opportunities within times of big change and upheaval, too.

Another way I practice creating a positive "Tetris" effect is to practice gratitude. This is a ubiquitous idea within the personal growth world, but I mention it here because it works. When we reflect on the things we're grateful for and/or express gratitude to someone else, we feel happier.

Expressing gratitude or thanking others for the positive influence they've had on our lives also helps us build relationships. The stronger our relationships are, the more support we have during transitions.

Some ways I practice gratitude include:

- Creating a doodle page in my journal and adding one word, phrase or doodle for each day of the month
- Writing a line a day on a dedicated page describing what I feel grateful for
- Making a list of "good things" every day—especially the small moments
- Keeping a digital photo journal of positive memories.

If this kind of practice doesn't come naturally to you, you might also consider doing something like artist Eli Trier. She spent a year writing thank-you notes to people who had touched or influenced her life. There is no "right" way to practice gratitude; it comes in many forms, shapes, and sizes. Experiment with focusing on the good in a way that feels right for you.

Practice your non-negotiables

Non-negotiables are the activities that help us feel like the best versions of ourselves. When we do them, our non-negotiables leave us with a sense of feeling grounded, peaceful, and fulfilled. When we do these things, life isn't easier, but we are better able to ride the waves as they come. Common non-negotiables include exercise, drinking enough water, journaling and spending time in nature. You can find a worksheet on how to make your own list of non-negotiables (what I call a "When Life Works" list; also see the chapter "How to Be Kind to Yourself When You're Feeling Blue") on the Resources page for this book at http://www.becomingwhoyouare.net/htbk-resources.

When we're going through a big transition and our attention is elsewhere, we tend to drop our non-negotiables to the bottom of our to-do lists. It is during these times more than ever, though, that we need to prioritize these activities. When we make time for the small rituals and routines that fill our cups, we give ourselves the best chance of thriving through the transition. We prevent ourselves from burning out, and set ourselves up to make decisions based on love rather than fear.

Check your coping mechanisms

At the same time as making space for my non-negotiables, I also pay attention to where I'm leaning a little too much on my coping mechanisms. Coping mechanisms are the go-to activities we use for comfort in the short term that don't serve our long-term health, happiness and wellbeing. Common candidates include over-eating, over-drinking, over-sleeping, over-spending, binge-watching on repeat, or some other excess. These things are tricky, because they can feel like self-care in the short term. But the difference between coping strategies and genuine self-care is that coping strategies stop us from feeling our actual feelings. When we rely on these things in the long term, we usually end up feeling worse. That's not to mention the negative consequences for our health, bank balance, and quality of life. You can find out more about transforming coping mechanisms into self-caring behaviors in my book, *From Coping to Thriving: How to Turn Self-Care Into a Way of Life*.

When we're in the middle of a stressful transition, we are susceptible to falling back on these coping mechanisms to get us through. I'm not suggesting we should all become teetotal, snack on kale, and spend our evenings live-streaming yoga classes instead of Netflix. Using our coping strategies consciously and temporarily is fine, as long as we're clear with ourselves. For tonight, we get to drink mojitos and eat pity pizza; come tomorrow, we get back out there. Boundaries are a form of self-kindness—especially boundaries with ourselves. We don't want to set up camp in pizza-and-mojito town and turn over-indulging into a regular way of dealing with uncomfortable feelings. It's a stop on the journey, not the destination. Give yourself a set amount of time to indulge, then get back to your non-negotiables and the things that light you up.

Accept that you're not functioning at 100% (and that it won't last forever)

During big transitions, one of the kindest things we can do is to accept reality. This means accepting we're in the middle of a big transition. It also means accepting our energy and attention are elsewhere and, while this is happening, we won't be functioning at 100%. We will need to postpone or cancel some things while we work this through. We will need extra support. And that's all OK.

Sometimes, we worry that if we give ourselves a break today, then that break will snowball out of control. We'll let everything drop tomorrow, the next day, and the day after that, until we end up in a big heap of apathetic failure. Sometimes we tell ourselves we should be able to deal with all this (after all, don't other people seem to?). The truth, however, is that we have finite energy. And if some of that energy is being taken up by a transition, then something else has to give in the meantime. It's much better to make a conscious decision about what that's going to be rather than try to plow on. If we do that, we're going to drop the balls we've been trying to juggle, and end up having that decision made for us by chance or circumstance.

I find that during and after big transitions, I need time to relax and take things easy. Often, it's not even optional. My mind becomes foggy. I want to do things with my hands rather than my brain, and I need time to decompress— even if it's just for a couple of hours. Trying to push through and continue business as usual doesn't work. If I try to make it work, the brain fog lasts for longer (remember the part about energy from How to Be Kind to Yourself When You're Finding it Hard to Get Motivated? It applies here too). Instead, I've found it most helpful to listen to that need for time out. With that in mind, I recognize this need won't last forever—if I feed that need, at some point I will get my mojo back.

Pay attention to what you can learn from the experience

Returning to the book *The Happiness Advantage*, psychologist Shawn Achor also talks about shifting our perspective. Rather than bouncing back from challenging or adverse situations, we want to focus on bouncing *forward*. The phrase "bouncing back" suggests we (and life) will return to being just as it was before the transition happened. If we're open to it, most transitions give us experience, new perspective, understanding, and resilience. I've found I have a more positive (or at least bearable) experience of challenging situations when I focus on what I can learn and how I can grow from them. This doesn't mean I have to like, welcome, or feel happy about the transition. Sweeping your true feelings about a situation under the psychological rug isn't helpful or healthy. But you can acknowledge a situation is hard and not one you would have chosen while also being aware of how you have bounced forward. In this way, it becomes an opportunity to learn more about yourself and how capable you are.

You've got this.

Your moment of kindness

Think of a transition you're experiencing in life at the moment. How can you use the "Tetris Effect" to your advantage?

What are your non-negotiables? (I've mentioned this earlier in the book, but if you're not sure, you can find a link to a free worksheet to help you identify yours on the Resources page of this book). And what are your go-to coping mechanisms?

When you think of transitions you've experienced in the past, how have you "bounced forward"?

How can you be 5% kinder to yourself today as you experience this transition?

TWENTY-FIVE
HOW TO BE KIND TO YOURSELF IN THE FACE OF JUDGMENT

Plant your own garden and decorate your own soul, instead of waiting for someone to bring you flowers.

—Veronica A. Shoffstall

A few years ago, I was talking with a friend about wanting to try something new at work and being sure—100% convinced!—that people would judge me. One of the great things about sharing stuff on the Internet is that someone somewhere is going to read it and have something to say in response. And one of the perils of sharing stuff on the Internet is that someone somewhere is going to read it and have something to say in response. I no longer remember the details of that new thing, but I remember the visceral sense of dread as I thought about the wave of negativity that would inevitably flow my way. My friend's response? "Most of the time people are too busy thinking about their own lives to notice what other people are doing and judge that."

Well, then. This is now my go-to reminder when I get stressed over judgment about tiny things. It's also a useful barometer for authenticity when I'm worrying about what other people think: What would I do if I knew other people wouldn't notice? Life coach Amy E. Smith suggested a similar thought experiment when I interviewed her. She explained she employs a technique she calls "Rock it out." It involves asking herself: if these people around me were all just rocks, how would I be behaving right now? It's a simple game, but it helps illuminate where we're changing our behavior through fear of judgment from others.

Still, the fear of judgment isn't irrational: judgment happens. It's part of being out in the world, living our lives. Chances are, at some point somewhere down the road, someone will judge or criticize us for something. And, at that moment, it won't feel good.

This is far more likely to happen now (and harder to ignore) thanks to the Internet and social media. While I love these things, I've also experienced the downside to online anonymity. A definite empathy gap arises from being behind a screen rather than face to face. A small but vocal minority are quick to attack, shame, criticize, and judge.

We've all heard the saying, "Sticks and stones may break my bones, but your words will never hurt me." But as gutsy as this might sound, the truth is words do hurt, and being vulnerable to that hurt doesn't make us weak or thin-skinned. It makes us human. Overcoming a fear of judgment is more about making peace with the fact judgment will happen at some point (and developing a self-kindness toolbox to deal with it) than about trying to avoid it.

How other people behave is a reflection on them

Let's start with a basic fact: other people's judgments of us are rarely only about us. This is much easier to digest and internalize when we're in a place of feeling calm and secure, so re-read that last sentence and let this sink in.

When we struggle with self-kindness, we often place more stock on what other people think of us. We look for validation and acceptance outside of ourselves. This makes it harder to separate out other people's thoughts, opinions and feelings about our choices and behavior from our own. In reality, many things affect people's judgments of you that have nothing to do with you. These range from their own histories, beliefs, and experiences, what's going on in their life right now, to the dodgy prawn sandwich they had for lunch. Everyone has responsibility for whether—and how—they choose to communicate their thoughts and feelings.

Although taking things personally is another human trait, we don't want to take responsibility for how other people behave. There might be truth within someone's judgments of us, but it's also worth stopping to reflect. How might their own experiences, beliefs, and internal stuff (i.e. things that are nothing to do with us) be contributing to this, too?

Not everyone's opinion is useful, relevant, or important (even if they think it is)

As we already looked at in "How to Be Kind to Yourself When the Urge to People-Please is Strong," who we internalize feedback from matters. Our personal boundaries exist to let the good in and keep the bad out. This includes knowing when to ignore, knowing when to say "Thanks," with a smile and move on, and knowing when to stop and listen.

Sometimes people are not kind, but there is truth in what they're saying and opportunities to learn from them. We don't want to install a blanket policy of only listening to positive feedback, because when we do that, we're not helping ourselves. I sometimes receive feedback about my writing or ideas that is uncomfortable, but valuable. I also receive feedback where it's clear the person has different expectations about what I should write and what opinions I should have. Neither of us is wrong, we're just on different wavelengths.

Feedback is a gift, and it's our choice whether we accept it. Defining this boundary is a lifelong process, but it starts with recognizing we have the freedom to choose.

Run through the best friend test

This is something I've already mentioned in "How to Be Kind to Yourself When You Make a Mistake." It's also useful in this context, so I'll include it here, too. Think of your best friend, or someone who most embodies kindness, compassion, and wisdom to you. What would they say to you in this situation? And what would you say to them if they were in your position? As we've already discussed, when we struggle with self-kindness, we can treat other people with more compassion than we offer ourselves. The best friend test helps us become more conscious of where we're short-changing ourselves so we can adjust accordingly.

Giving yourself a hug

We talked about the sympathetic and parasympathetic systems in "How to Be Kind to Yourself When You're Feeling Overwhelmed." Slowing our breathing helps us shift from the "fight-or-flight" response of the sympathetic nervous system to the "rest and digest" mode of the parasympathetic nervous system. Giving ourselves a hug—yes, an actual, genuine hug—takes that principle a step further. This suggestion comes from Kristin Neff's excellent book *Self-Compassion: Stop Beating Yourself Up and Leave Insecurity Behind*. Our nervous system responds to touch, and anything tactile, like a hug or even brushing our hair, can release oxytocin, also known as the love hormone. Wrapping our arms around ourselves while channeling feelings of compassion offers similar comfort to receiving a hug from someone else (although this is also a good option if someone huggable is present and willing).

Explore and soften the old wounds

More often than not, the things people say hurt us because they plug into wounds that already exist. Whether the person on the other end of the interaction means to poke at old sore points or not, these experiences can trigger old insecurities. The more we can explore and soften the old wounds that re-emerge when people aren't kind, the more we can choose to show that kindness to ourselves. The more we can explore what our needs are in relation to these wounds, the more we can meet these needs in the present. None of these options involve the other person changing their behavior. We're responsible for our own feelings and responses, and that's a good thing, because it's the only thing we can alter in these situations. Showing ourselves compassion and kindness, even when other people don't, is one of the greatest gifts we can give ourselves.

Say something

Sometimes self-kindness and meeting old needs involve speaking up. The other person might not realize how their words or actions are landing with you. Or, they might well do, but you might still want to advocate for yourself and say "enough." As well as offering ourselves internal comfort, self-kindness involves advocating for ourselves. We might want someone else to come along and defend us, or think the other person should realize the effects of their words and actions. But no one cares as much about our emotional wellbeing as we do. It's up to us.

In most situations, the best way to speak up is with a clear and specific request. "Please don't make jokes about my weight," "I'm happy with the way I dress; if you continue to criticize my appearance, this conversation will be over." Up to a point, we teach people how to treat us. We cannot control (nor are we responsible for) other people's behavior, but clear and concise boundaries are part of practicing self-kindness.

This isn't a license to be unkind toward the other person. One of my biggest defenses is sarcasm. Left unchecked, this is my go-to mode of communication when someone does or says something that leaves me feeling hurt and/or angry. On one level, it's an attempt to make them feel the way I do. It's also a cheap shot. I don't feel good about it later, and it's not aligned with the person I want to be, so it's better to resist the urge to snark. Whenever we respond to someone in a challenging situation, it helps to check in with ourselves before doing so. We can ask, "Does this response bring me closer to or take me further away from the person I want to be?"

If necessary, walk away

As I've already mentioned, we cannot change other people. We can only change our response to other people. If we speak up, stand our ground and the person or people in question continue to be unkind, it might be time for some distance. Walking away is a last resort, and it's difficult to do. But it sends a powerful message to ourselves and others. You don't tolerate unnecessary unkindness, and you won't enable the other person to continue behaving in that way, either.

In this chapter, we've explored self-kindness in the face of judgment. The next chapter continues this theme with a related topic: rejection. Yes, that uncomfortable experience that we'd all rather avoid, but is an inevitable part of being alive. It's not all bad, though; there are steps we can take to be on our own side, even when it feels like other people aren't. We'll explore this more in the next few pages.

Your moment of kindness:

Think of a time when you were on the receiving end of someone's judgments. How would you respond differently if you were to respond from a place of self-kindness?

TWENTY-SIX
HOW TO BE KIND TO YOURSELF IN THE FACE OF REJECTION

To be yourself in a world that is constantly trying to make you something else is the greatest accomplishment.

—Ralph Waldo Emerson

She felt wounded.

It was heartache.

The sting of rejection.

Her words cut deep.

What does rejection feel like to you? The phrases we use to describe the experience of rejection often compare it to physical pain, and this reflects how visceral rejection can feel. Although the subject is up for debate in the scientific community, some research has shown that experiencing social rejection does, in fact, stimulate similar areas in the brain as physical pain. Whether or not this is actually the case, if you've ever felt rejection, you'll know it feels like the statements above and much more.

Why is self-kindness in the face of rejection so hard? Because rejection seems like a refusal of acceptance and belonging. We are social animals, and we need a stable community of people around us to feel secure. Most of us also somewhat base our perception of ourselves on the feedback we receive from other people. This means when someone rejects us—whether it's in conversation, for a date, for a job, or otherwise—it momentarily calls our place in this world into question. We are being cast out or refused acceptance to the tribe. Ancestrally and in childhood, being cast out of a group carried bigger stakes than not getting a date or a shiny corner office. Rejection left us to fend for ourselves, left us more vulnerable and less likely to survive.

While the nomadic tribal days of our ancestors are over and we're all grown up (-ish), the hard-wiring that makes rejection push our internal "Emergency!" button still exists. Rejection also poses an existential threat. Experiencing rejection can lead to shame, feelings of isolation and alienation, and all the emotions that come with that. These include frustration, anger, and a kind of pain that can feel like a deep emotional wound.

As Brené Brown explains in her book, *I Thought It Was Just Me (But it Isn't)*, the experience of shame can trigger one of five responses. Without being conscious of our reactions, most of us respond to rejection in one or more of the following ways:

1. We assume the person, people, or organization rejecting us are correct. There is something deficient or wrong with us and we deserved the

rejection. We turn our "fight" response toward ourselves.

2. We assume the person, people, or organization rejecting us are in the wrong. We focus on and react to this as a way of avoiding feeling the uncomfortable feelings rejection can provoke. We turn our "fight" response toward others.
3. We detach from the feelings associated with rejection, telling ourselves it's all part of "toughening up." Given that emotions aren't a pick-n-mix, this usually means detaching from all our feelings. We freeze.
4. We crumble, retreat to lick our wounds, and try to avoid potential rejection in the future. Flight.

Recently, psychologists have also suggested a fourth addition to this framework: "fawn." This describes the desire to please or appease in response to feelings of shame. With rejection, this might look like trying to win approval from the person or people who have rejected us. These are all automatic, unconscious responses from a powerful yet primitive part of our brain (often called the "lizard brain"). Often, these responses are rooted in experiences that can date back to childhood. Luckily, we also have other parts of our brain, namely the limbic system and neocortex, that can help us rationalize and temper the effects of the lizard brain.

So how can we approach painful, embarrassing, or shame-inducing rejections from a place of self-kindness?

Prepare a list in advance of ways you can be kind to yourself in the face of rejection

I don't know about you, but making kind decisions when I am already feeling overwhelmed, lonely and ashamed is near-impossible. Create a list in advance of the kindest things you can do for yourself when you experience rejection. With this list, you give yourself a much better chance of self-kindness when the time comes. And it will come; rejection is a natural part of life. Your list might include:

- Activities you find soothing
- Trusted confidantes you can turn to for advice and support
- Mantras you find helpful to remember during hard times
- Favorite places that hold positive memories and lift your spirits

Step away from the story

Much of the hurt and pain we experience comes not from the rejection itself, but from the meanings we attach to the rejection. In a later book, *Rising Strong*, Brené Brown shares the work of neurologist Robert Burton. He explains why jumping to conclusions is so tempting, even when we know better. According to Burton, our brains reward us with dopamine whenever we recognize and complete patterns, whenever we fill in the gaps and reach an understanding about something. The problem is, we don't have to be right to get this dopamine hit: we just need to *think* we're right. Certainty matters more than accuracy.

And this is where we run into issues with our stories. It's why, when a friend doesn't respond to a call or email, we think "She must be mad at me about something." We feel a sense of satisfaction from thinking this, even though the idea also provokes anxiety and upset. The story is complete, and we have answered the question of why she hasn't responded. Ping: dopamine hit. So, how do we temper the urge to race to a conclusion and instead focus on responding, rather than reacting?

First, by noticing when we're doing it. Our stories often feel justified and very real, so this part can be tricky. But the sooner we can accept that we're wired to fill in the gaps and complete the puzzle, the sooner we can become more aware of which pieces we're using to do this. This includes the story we tell ourselves about our stories. Remember the two arrows parable I shared in the introduction to this book? Beating ourselves up when we realize we've attached a story to a rejection is that second arrow.

We can separate fact from fiction by prioritizing asking questions over finding answers, by asking "What do I *know* to be true here?" We can also look at the feelings underneath our response. Feelings like anger often mask other feelings, like vulnerability, shame, guilt, and so on. When we can name those underlying feelings, we can better address them. And, when we can recognize and accept that sometimes we don't—and won't—know, that becomes our new certainty.

Questions to ask include:

What are the facts of the situation?

Can you describe what happened as objectively as possible? For example, story: *Suzy ignored me on the street.*

Factual account: *I waved to Suzy on the street. She carried on walking and didn't return my greeting.*

While it might have been easy to assume Suzy ignored me, I don't know that for sure right now. This might seem like semantics, but facts are neutral and assumption-free. Anything more is a story.

What is my interpretation of the situation?

This is where you get to run wild with your worst-case scenarios: *Suzy deliberately ignored me because she doesn't like me. In fact, she's never liked me, she's always thought I was stuffy and uptight. And now she's not even pretending to be my friend, she's probably been talking to all our mutual friends behind my back about how boring I am. You know what? Screw Suzy!*

Interesting. Hold that thought; don't buy into it as truth or judge it as ridiculous/over the top/evidence there is something wrong with you. Let it sit there and move on to the next question.

What are other interpretations of the situation that I haven't yet considered?

With this question, we have the chance to practice empathy for other people and step into their shoes for a few minutes. *Suzy might not have seen me waving. She might have been lost in thought and not realized it was me. She might have seen me, but been dealing with something else and not felt like stopping to chat.*

When you consider these possibilities, how do you feel about the situation now?

How do these questions shift your thoughts and feelings about the situation? How do you feel about Suzy now? And how do you feel about yourself?

What would you tell a friend in this situation?

Ah, the old best friend test again. We usually find it easier to offer kindness to other people because we have a different perspective on their situation.

To use this to your advantage, ask yourself: *What would I say to my best friend, and how can I apply this same compassion to myself?*

Celebrate the fact you went there

Whether your rejection followed inviting a new friend for coffee, telling someone you love them, or applying for the job of your dreams, you put yourself out there and you went for it. Regardless of the outcome, you deserve a massive round of applause for showing up and doing it.

When someone rejects us, it means the situation in't right for us. No matter how much we wanted that relationship, partnership, or arrangement, it's not a good match—right now, anyway. As painful as it can be in the short term, in the long run, rejection is a kindness. You read that right: rejection is a kindness. When people refuse us, they're not only being real with us, but they are also making room in our lives for people and situations that are a better fit.

Common inner critic counterarguments

One of the tricky things about rejection is that it is great at activating our inner critics. With that in mind, I want to use the rest of this chapter to address some questions and comments this voice often uses to push back:

But what if other people are right and there really is something wrong with me?

Whether or not we're aware of it, we filter our experiences through how we already see ourselves. When we struggle with self-kindness, we are quick to hoard negative comments while dismissing or overlooking the positive feedback. We talked about this as "The Tetris Effect" in "How to Be Kind to Yourself in the Middle of Big Transitions." Psychologists call this negativity bias, and it feeds our sense there is something wrong with us. In reality, though, the truth is far more balanced and nuanced than our inner negativity-hoarder would have us believe. Yes, there are things we can all improve about ourselves—and there are lots of positive things to treasure about ourselves, too.

Just because someone else makes a judgment about us, it doesn't mean they're right. Whether we accept someone's opinion as an accurate reflection of who we are is our decision. This is where self-kindness and self-awareness form a virtuous circle. The more we know and accept ourselves, the more we can distinguish between helpful criticism and unhelpful criticism. We can hear what people say without internalizing their words as truth. At the other end of the spectrum, we can listen without closing ourselves off to feedback or reflection.

Even if there is an element of truth in what someone says about you, there is nothing "wrong" with you that you can't work with, change, or learn to accept with the right approach and support. As I've mentioned in previous chapters, we're all in a constant process of developing as people. Just like the human race has evolved to where it currently stands today, we're always growing as individuals. Reflecting on the right kind of feedback is an important part of that growth.

But what if I get stuck? No one likes a dweller; isn't onward and upward the best approach?

Yes, and no. Neither rumination nor dissociation, the two extremes in this context, is helpful. Instead, the optimal (and kindest) path lies somewhere in the middle.

Rumination involves replaying a situation over and over in our minds, with little development in our perspective, thoughts, or feelings. When we ruminate, we set ourselves up to re-experience the rejection repeatedly. This can leave us in near-constant pain, feeling bitter and stuck. Rumination is deceptive. It can sometimes feel like we're working through the issue, especially if we're using tools like journaling or therapy. The difference is when these things are helping, we experience a shift in our feelings and understanding. With rumination, we don't. Dissociating or distancing ourselves from our feelings isn't helpful, either. As I mentioned earlier in this chapter (and in "How to Be Kind to Yourself When 'Self-Love' Feels Unrelatable"), we can't pick our emotions. When we cut ourselves off from one feeling, we cut ourselves off from other feelings too—including joy, happiness, excitement, love, and more.

The middle ground involves acknowledging your feelings while working to process them constructively. There's a difference between allowing yourself to feel the pain associated with rejection and launching into full-on rumination mode. We don't want to live in the land of victimhood, but we need to accept what we're feeling to move forward. It's important to show ourselves compassion, and it's also important to ask questions like, "What did I learn from this?" "What could I do differently next time?" "How could I respond to a similar situation if it happens again?"

But if there's nothing wrong with me yet someone has rejected me, then why wouldn't I think they are wrong?

A rejection is a refusal, and refusals happen for lots of reasons. When we unpack the assumption that if someone refuses us they are wrong, we often find masked hurt or fear underneath. If we stay in a place of blame or judgment, all we're doing is offloading the energy that comes with uncomfortable emotions onto someone else. We're not allowing ourselves to feel our genuine feelings, nor are we being fair to the other person or people involved. When we allow ourselves to feel our feelings and acknowledge there could be many reasons why the situation turned out this way, we are more likely to process the situation and move forward.

For most of us, the experience of rejection (and most of the experiences I've included in this book) is not fun or easy to go through. While I hope the preceding chapters have been helpful, I'm aware can't cover individually the many experiences that challenge our self-kindness. With that in mind, the next chapter offers a few general thoughts and suggestions about how to be kind to yourself when bad things happen.

Your moment of kindness:

How are you going to be kind to yourself in the face of rejection from now on? Take a few moments and visualize what this might look like now.

TWENTY-SEVEN
HOW TO BE KIND TO YOURSELF WHEN BAD THINGS HAPPEN

---

and here you are living

despite it all

—Rupi Kaur, *The Sun and Her Flowers*

Illness, redundancy, breakups, loss, discrimination, challenging world events. Bad things happen to us all at some point. How can we practice self-kindness when we're reeling from bad news or a traumatic experience, or are knee-deep in a hard, ongoing situation? In this chapter, I want to share a few suggestions that go deeper than the general advice to "stay positive." As with each chapter in this book, I'm aware I'm writing this from one perspective only. I don't know what you've experienced or what bad things you might think of as you read this chapter. Neither am I writing this with the assumption that I can relate to what you're experiencing or can provide the one piece of advice that will fix it. So I invite you to take the suggestions below that work for you and adapt or leave those that don't.

Focus on what you can control, leave what you can't

I've mentioned this idea before, but I'm including it here again. It's important and, if you're like me, you might need a few reminders before it sinks in. So here is that reminder: when bad things happen, focus on what you can control and where you can make a difference. This might not solve "the problem," but know that in your own way, you are making a difference. If you're concerned about the environment, what is one thing you can start doing in your daily life that will make your personal impact more positive? If you disagree with the actions of politicians, higher government, or something else that is ultimately beyond your sphere of control, what is one thing you can do to live by your values and what matters to you in your own life?

Focusing on what we can't control is attractive, as it gives us a sense of power where we feel powerless. It also takes our energy and attention away from what we *can* control and influence. And there's the rub. Focusing on what we can't control makes us less effective and can leave us feeling even more helpless, disempowered, and hopeless. The more time and energy we're spending on the things we can't control, the less time and energy we're spending on the ways in which we can make a difference.

A reflective exercise

If you're dealing with uncertainty in a particular area of life right now, try using the questions below to clarify where you have control, where you don't, and how to focus on what matters.

1. Think of an ongoing unresolved situation in your life. Write an outline of the facts and why it feels unresolved for you.

2. What can you control in this situation? Make a list.

3. What can't you control in this situation? Make a list.

4. Being honest with yourself, on which of the above things are you spending most of your energy and attention right now?

5. How can you focus more on the things you can control? What would that look like?

Avoid Spiritual Bypassing (from yourself or others) and recognize your feelings as valid

Chances are you've come across one of the following phrases:

Everything happens for a reason.

Good vibes only!

You create your own reality.

It's all part of God's plan.

It will happen for you if you want it enough.

Phrases like these usually come from a well-meaning place. What they all have in common, though, is they use spiritual or pseudo-spiritual "truths" to sidestep feelings. In the world of spiritual bypassing, pain, anger, hurt, grief, disappointment, regret, and other so-called negative emotions are things we should let go of ASAP. Like most things that fall under the category "self-help gone bad," spiritual bypassing has some basis in truth. Reliving an upsetting event on repeat isn't helpful or emotionally healthy. But neither is trying to bypass those feelings and skip straight to the part where it's all sunshine and unicorns. Part of the issue with these kinds of statements is that they deny the upsetting reality of what has happened. They deny the person's emotional response and shut down crucial pathways to understanding and healing. I understand the urge to do this, and I'm not immune to spreading these kinds of messages myself.

Even though I have over a decade's experience working in emotional support—even though I know better—I hear someone talk about a challenge or issue and I want to help, but I don't know what to say. I want them to feel better, partly for them but partly because seeing them in pain feels uncomfortable for me. At these times, I have to bite my tongue to stop myself from coming out with one of the pithy platitudes that annoy me when I hear them from other people. Witnessing someone else's pain requires a vulnerability that can be uncomfortable. Part of me aches to jump in and try to rescue them and make it all better underneath a flashing neon sign that reads "Good vibes only!" This is spiritual bypassing.

Many mental health professionals have written and spoken about the damage spiritual bypassing can do. Writing for his website, Robert Masters explains spiritual bypassing can manifest as numbing our feelings; overemphasizing the positive; celebrating excessive detachment; an anti-anger stance; a sense that one is more enlightened than others who experience such "negative" emotions, and more. Psychologist Ingrid Clayton emphasizes that spiritual bypassing is a subtle but effective defense mechanism. She writes, "Spiritual bypass shields us from the truth, it disconnects us from our feelings, and helps us avoid the big picture. It is more about checking *out* than checking in."

The idea we can "cure" ourselves of negative thoughts and feelings isn't helpful or necessary. Negative thoughts and feelings serve a purpose. They alert us to things in our life that are not working. This might be a relationship that isn't working. It might be the fact you're grieving a significant loss. Maybe you need to make changes in your life (or at least the way you're thinking about your life).

As I mentioned earlier in this book, these feelings make up an important part of our internal GPS—our intuition. This is our felt sense of the world based on previous experiences, our beliefs, and information we have registered on an unconscious level. Our intuition doesn't always reflect the truth, but it's worth paying attention to.

Spiritual bypassing is like driving to a destination with the belief that turning left is the unenlightened choice, so we won't do it. If each time the GPS tells us to turn left, we say "Oh, you don't mean that," and go another way instead, we're very unlikely to end up where we want to go. Negative feelings and thoughts are the "turn left" of our internal GPS. They contain important information about ourselves and the world. They are part of being human. And, as a bonus, they make the sweeter moments even sweeter.

The alternative to spiritual bypassing is simple—not easy, but simple. It is to *feel our feelings* (when that's helpful… more on that below). It also involves acknowledging what Walt Whitman writes in his poem "Song of Myself": "I am large, I contain multitudes." We're allowed to have conflicting feelings about ourselves, our experiences and the world. We can feel grateful and sad, grief and relief, anger and hope, all at the same time. It involves being willing to notice all the feelings that come up. This includes the uncomfortable or so-called unacceptable emotions. It also involves acknowledging those feelings are as valid as any other. It includes accepting the reality of a situation:

This feels hard, it feels heavy, it feels impossible. It's also acknowledging these feelings are fleeting and will probably ease over time. Finally, it involves acknowledging our feelings in responses to situations that aren't about us. The times when we experience the urge to jump in and rescue someone. The times we want to shut down their pain because we feel uncomfortable witnessing it. Being willing to sit, listen, and *be* instead of *do* time and time again.

Self-kindness involves embracing all our feelings. Kindness toward others involves allowing them to do the same.

Give yourself time

Many years ago, I was mugged while abroad. It was scary, violating, and left me feeling helpless and disempowered. I was lucky (and grateful) nothing more serious happened beyond theft and the threat of violence. But the experience shook me. Mundane activities like going to the local bus station became overwhelming. Even though I knew I had been in the wrong place at the wrong time and the chances of it happening again were slim, part of me was convinced something bad was going to happen again. I would be out of control, someone would catch me unawares, and I wouldn't be able to stop them taking something or doing something to me. I tried everything to make these heavy feelings go away. I wanted to enjoy the rest of my time where I was, not spend it scared to even put one foot out the front door. I journaled about it; I talked about it; I tried to challenge my fears, but in the end, what helped the most was time. Gradually, the fear dissipated. I went from thinking about it many times a day to a few times a day, then less. Almost ten years later, I can't even remember the last time I thought about it.

As clichéd as it sounds, sometimes time is the best healer. I say sometimes, because sometimes it's also not, and in these situations we need extra support or help to process what has happened. But this experience was a good lesson for me in dealing with loss, grief, and hard experiences that have happened since then: give it time. Give yourself time. There is no rule that says you should be back to "normal" (whatever that means) within a certain timeframe. Get support if you need it, but start with acceptance for yourself and your experience without the pressure to be fine before you're ready.

Give yourself space

You don't have to feel your feelings 100% of the time, especially if it's overwhelming or becoming too much and you also need to function in the world. You are allowed to distract yourself, to switch off, and to do things that will lessen the intensity for a while if it feels too much. As psychotherapist Seerut K. Chawla points out, forcing ourselves to feel feelings we're not ready to feel is akin to repeatedly poking a bruise. It won't help us heal: "Sometimes healing means knowing to leave some things alone."

This is not the same as avoiding feelings. You're not taking a blanket approach to dismiss every feeling you experience. Rather, you're taking care of your own wellbeing in the face of challenging or overwhelming emotions. Avoiding feelings often looks like channeling that energy into activities that aren't good for us or don't support our future wellbeing (in my book *From Coping to Thriving: How to Turn Self-Care Into a Way of Life* I talk more about coping mechanisms and the alternatives to them). Everyone responds differently to difficult situations and challenging circumstances. There is no prescriptive approach that will be right for everyone. But, if you have been pushing yourself to sit with big feelings and it's not helping, what would happen if you backed off for a while? As the saying goes, if trying harder isn't working, maybe it's time to try softer. On a related note…

Get support (if you want and/or need it)

You don't have to go through hard things alone. Not only that, but your hard thing doesn't have to meet a minimum criteria to be worthy of support. We aren't all competing for gold in the "Who has it worst" olympics. I didn't need professional support after the mugging experience I wrote about earlier in this chapter. Something else happened a couple of years after that, though, that was much less traumatic, involved no violence, and was a slow-burning situation rather than "Bam! Now you're being mugged." It knocked me for six emotionally. That time, I needed extra support and went back to counseling for a few months—something that was incredibly helpful.

Support might look like professional therapy, but it doesn't have to. It might be talking to a trusted friend or reading a book about what you're dealing with. It even might be following people who are saying what you need to hear on social media (and unfollowing or muting those who are saying what you don't need to hear right now).

Take a media break

This is especially the case if the bad thing is something that's happened in the larger world. Media—digital, physical, and social—thrives on bad news, crises, and provoking feelings of fear, panic, and scarcity. Bad news sells. Scaremongering headlines are more likely to shift copies or get clicks than those that say, "It's not as bad as it seems."

Yes, there is something to be said for staying connected so you know what's happening. At the beginning of the coronavirus pandemic, when England's Government announced a sudden nationwide lockdown, I was glued to the news, tracking updates, cases and deaths. For a day or two, this helped me feel in control. I wanted answers to my questions: How bad was this? How long was the lockdown going to go on for? Was the health system going to collapse? And, more immediately, when would we be able to buy toilet roll again? After a while, though, my news-scanning became doom-scrolling. It left me feeling more helpless (see the point above about focusing on what we can control) and it wasn't helping me to do the things I needed to do to get by each day. As with all these suggestions, you know yourself best. You know deep down when it's better for you to stay connected versus when it's in your best interests to disconnect and switch off the noise temporarily.

Start with one thing

If you're finding it hard not to feel overwhelmed by everything happening in the world right now, keep it simple. Choose one cause or mission you will focus on in your life and decide on one to three changes you will make in your life today to support that cause. This isn't about ignoring other issues in the world, but it's about doing what you can, when you can, in a way that's sustainable for you.

Before you try to save the world, you need to save yourself. If the bad thing has left you feeling like life is falling apart around you, the next chapter is for you. In the meantime, here are a few questions for you:

Your moment of kindness:

How can you be 10% kinder to yourself when bad things happen?

What actions will you take?

What can you prepare now?

TWENTY-EIGHT
HOW TO BE KIND TO YOURSELF WHEN LIFE FEELS LIKE IT'S FALLING APART

> The very least you can do in your life is figure out what you hope for. And the most you can do is live inside that hope.
>
> —Barbara Kingsolver

You're in it: that dark, muddy place where life feels like it's falling apart. Perhaps you've experienced a single life-changing event that's catapulted you into change. Perhaps it's been a slow slide downwards to where you can't see a way back.

Whatever's happening, I know life hasn't always felt like it's falling apart, but I trust there are good reasons it does right now.

The thing we forget—that I forget and I wonder if you've forgotten right now, too—is that we've been here before. Maybe not in quite the same way, but we've been at our "bottom." We've experienced times when it didn't feel like things could get any worse.

And yet you have this amazing track record behind you.

When life feels like it's falling apart, remember this: *you've made it through, 100% of the time.*

When life feels like it's falling apart, it's easy to focus on all the things that are wrong, bad, lacking, destroyed, gone, lost, betrayed, and forsaken.

But among all those things are the many things that are not.

The things that remain. The breeze on your skin. That song you love to listen to. All the kind words and meaningful moments you've collected over the years. All the successes, small wins, hard things you've done. You are still here and you're still moving forward.

And there are those days you've made it through, even if they feel like a distant memory right now. So far, you have a 100% success rate of making it through those days. Congratulations! I don't know about you, but I look at some of the darkest moments from my past and I think "Yes, that's an achievement."

And when I look back at the previous chapters of my life, I realize everything ebbs and flows. Just like winter, spring, summer, and fall march onward, cycling forward, so do we, and this too will pass. Even if this is the worst thing, unlike anything you've ever faced before, think back to the last time you felt this way: you made it through. You'll make it through again, and you'll raise that bar of resilience and self-trust for the future.

Wherever you are right now, it might not be pleasant, it might not be fun, you might not see a way out (yet), but here's what you've proven countless times before:

You've got this.

Take a deep breath and ride the wave.

Your moment of kindness:

What have you made it through?

What does this show about your strength and resilience?

WHAT COMES NEXT?

I hope this book has been helpful as you reflect on how to be kinder to yourself when it feels hardest.

Now, the hard work begins. At a basic level, being mean to ourselves is a habit. It's a well-worn neural pathway honed over years of practice. Each time we choose self-criticism, we make that pathway a little stronger. Yet, no matter strong that pathway becomes, we can always choose to take a different path next time. In the beginning, that might look like journeying down the original path of self-criticism. Then we realize hours, days, months later that this is where we've gone. We ask ourselves, "what might it look like to live that situation again with self-compassion?" It might look like realizing we're in the middle of that well-worn path as we're on it, as the self-criticism is happening. Time to try again. The more we practice this reset, the easier it becomes. The more we go back and try something different and kinder—however imperfect—the more accessible we make other pathways. Eventually, the old self-critical path becomes rugged and weedy, and not especially easy to traverse. The kinder path becomes the familiar, well-worn route we can travel down with more ease.

Self-kindness is not a grand gesture, but 1,000 tiny thoughts and actions scattered throughout our day. It's a glass of water; sitting down for a few moments; saying no; saying yes; putting down our phones; eating when we're hungry; questioning a thought or feeling instead of jumping straight into judgment; asking ourselves, "What do I think of this person?" instead of worrying about what they think of us; holding ourselves accountable to do the things we say we're going to do; pushing ourselves to finish something even though we don't feel like it, because we know it's in our best interests to keep going; leaving a long-held commitment or path behind because we realize it's in our best interests to stop.

Being kind to ourselves isn't a onetime action. It's an ongoing practice. The more we practice it, the more natural it will feel, but it requires time, patience, and awareness. It's a moment-by-moment process. Self-kindness takes time and mental energy. Although it becomes easier over time, it might always take conscious thought. The siren song of self-criticism can be strong.

Whatever your relationship with yourself has been like to this point, the only thing that matters now is what you choose to do next.

In case you need to hear it one more time: you've got this.

THANKS FOR READING THIS BOOK

I hope you've enjoyed it and have found it useful as you cultivate a kinder relationship with yourself. If you'd like to access the resources, book recommendations and video classes I mentioned in this book, you can find them on the Resources page here: http://www.becomingwhoyouare.net/htbk-resources.

If you enjoyed this book, please consider sharing a review on Amazon, Goodreads, or the website from which you purchased your copy. This doesn't have to be long—a couple of sentences is perfect. Your reviews are invaluable for independent authors like me and will help other potential readers decide if this book is right for them. If you have any comments or suggestions about this book, I would love to hear more about your experience. Feel free to get in touch with me and share your thoughts: hannah@becomingwhoyouare.net.

BIBLIOGRAPHY

Please note: you can find live links to the books, articles, and resources mentioned in this book (including those below) at http://www.becomingwhoyouare.net/htbk-resources

Achor, Shawn, *The Happiness Advantage*. Virgin Books, 2011.

Allen, David, *Getting Things Done: The Art of Stress-Free Productivity*. Piatkus, 2015.

Aurelius, Marcus, *Meditations*. Penguin Classics, 2006.

Beatty, Melodie, *Stop Being Mean to Yourself: A Story About Finding the True Meaning of Self-Love*. HarperOne, 2013.

Braime, Hannah, *The Power of Self-Kindness: How to Transform Your Relationship With Your Inner Critic*. Individuate Press, 2019.

Braime, Hannah, *From Coping to Thriving: How to Turn Self-Care Into a Way of Life*. Individuate Press, 2013.

Branden, Nathaniel, *The Six Pillars of Self-Esteem*. Random House USA Inc, 1995.

Brown, Brené, *I Thought It Was Just Me (But it Isn't)*. JP Tarcher/Penguin Putnam, 2008.

Brown, Brené, *The Gifts of Imperfection*. Hazelden Publishing, 2010.

Brown, Brené, *Daring Greatly: How the Courage to Be Vulnerable Transforms the Way We Live, Love, Parent, and Lead*. Penguin, 2013.

Brown, Brené, *Rising Strong*. Vermilion, 2015.

Cameron, Julia, *The Artist's Way*. Tarcherperigee, 2002.

Chawla, Seerut K., "Home page". https://www.seerutkchawla.com/.

Chodron, Pema, *When Things fall Apart: Heart Advice for Difficult Times*. Element, 2013.

Clayton, Ingrid, "Beware of Spiritual Bypass." Psychology Today. October 2, 2011. https://www.psychologytoday.com/blog/emotional-sobriety/201110/beware-spiritual-bypass

Cuddy, Amy, "Your Body Language May Shape Who You Are." TEDGlobal 2012. https://www.ted.com/talks/amy_cuddy_your_body_language_may_shape_who_you_are.

Di Pirro, Dani, "Positively Present". https://positivelypresent.com/.

Gilbert, Elizabeth, *Big Magic: Creative Living Beyond Fear*. Bloomsbury Publishing, 2015.

Katherine, Anne, *Where to Draw the Line: How to Set Healthy Boundaries Every Day*. Simon & Schuster Australia, 2000.

Maisel, Eric, "Can You Manage to Still Care?" The Good Men Project. January 30, 2021. https://goodmenproject.-

com/featured-content/can-you-manage-to-still-care-kpkn/.

Masters, Robert, "Spiritual Bypassing: Avoidance in Holy Drag." Robert Masters. https://www.robertmasters.com/2013/04/29/spiritual-bypassing/

Mischel, W., and E. B. Ebbesen, "Attention in Delay of Gratification." *Journal of Personality and Social Psychology*, 16(2), 1970, pp. 329–337. https://doi.org/10.1037/h0029815

Mohr, Tara, *Playing Big: A Practical Guide for Brilliant Women Like You*. Arrow, 2015.

Neff, Kristin, *Self-Compassion: Stop Beating Yourself Up and Leave Insecurity Behind*. Yellow Kite, 2011.

Palmer, Amanda, "The Art of Asking." TED2013. https://www.ted.com/talks/amanda_palmer_the_art_of_asking

Pressfield, Steven, *The War of Art: Break Through the Blocks and Win Your Inner Creative Battles*. Black Irish Entertainment LLC, 2012.

Przybylskia, Andrew K. et al., "Motivational, Emotional, and Behavioral Correlates of Fear of Missing Out." *Computers in Human Behavior* 29(4), July 2013, pp. 1841-1848. https://doi.org/10.1016/j.chb.2013.02.014

Schwartz, Tony, *The Way We're Working Isn't Working*. Simon & Schuster UK, 2016.

Soutscheck, Alexander et al., "Brain stimulation reveals crucial role of overcoming self-centeredness in self-control." *Science Advances* 2(10), October 2016. https://doi.org/10.1126/sciadv.1600992

Tracy, Brian, *Eat That Frog!: Get More Of The Important Things Done Today*. Hodder Paperbacks, 2013.

Wiseman, Richard, *The Luck Factor: The Scientific Study of the Lucky Mind*. Arrow, 2004.

Whitman, Walt. "Song of Myself (1892 Version)." Poetry Foundation. Accessed September 24, 2021. https://www.poetryfoundation.org/poems/45477/song-of-myself-1892-version

ALSO BY HANNAH BRAIME

The Ultimate Guide to Journaling

From Coping to Thriving: How to Turn Self-Care Into a Way of Life

The Power of Self-Kindness: How to Transform Your Relationship with Your Inner Critic

The Year of You: 365 Journal Writing Prompts for Creative Self-Discovery

The Year of You for Mothers: 365 Journal-Writing Prompts for Self-Reflection, Self-Care and Self-Discovery

The Year of You for Creatives: 365 Journal-Writing Prompts for Doing Your Best Creative Work

ABOUT THE AUTHOR

Hannah Braime is a creative coach and author, who writes about journaling, self-care, and creativity. She is the author of several other books, including *The Ultimate Guide to Journaling, The Year of You,* and *From Coping to Thriving: How to Turn Self-Care Into a Way of Life*. She also shares practical psychology-based articles and resources on creating a full and meaningful life with greater courage, compassion, and authenticity at www.becomingwhoyouare.net.

Stay in touch to hear more about future books:
www.becomingwhoyouare.net
hannah@becomingwhoyouare.net

www.ingramcontent.com/pod-product-compliance
Lightning Source LLC
Chambersburg PA
CBHW072050110526
44590CB00018B/3105